ROCKING THE CRADLE

Gillian E. Hanscombe and Jackie Forster

Rocking the Cradle

Lesbian Mothers:
A Challenge in Family Living

Alyson Publications, Inc. • Boston

This is a paperback original by Alyson Publications, Inc., PO Box 2783,
Boston, Mass. 02208. This is the first U.S. publication of *Rocking the
Cradle*. It was previously published in Great Britain, in a cloth edition,
by Peter Owen Limited, of London.

First U.S. printing: March 1982

ISBN 0 932870 17 1

Also by Gillian E. Hanscombe:

Between Friends (Alyson, 1982)

Contents

Preface

The usual idea of a lesbian is of someone you wouldn't really like to take home to tea with your mother, someone who isn't quite nice, someone who is possibly mad, or possibly dangerous, or possibly freakish and pitiable. In films and books she is nearly always shown as a very masculine-looking woman, who wears unfashionable clothes, or even men's clothes, who has a short back-and-sides, a hairy face, and flat, heavy shoes. To go with this image of a half-man, she is usually supposed to have a gruff voice and a flat bosom, to be overweight and somehow dirty-looking. This idea is so fixed in the popular mind that the word 'lesbian' itself is very often used as a term of abuse, and people imagine that no real woman, no nice woman, could be anything but hurt and insulted if you called her a lesbian. And what most adults pass on to their children is the feeling that a lesbian does something unmentionable and dreadful with another woman when they are alone and naked together. More sophisticated people, who also fear lesbians, think that these dreadful acts obsess the lesbian mind, which they think is, after all, a twisted, perverted, abnormal mind, so that lesbians are people whom any normal woman should be afraid of and from whom little girls should be kept away.

It will seem strange to many, therefore, to hear that hundreds of lesbians are not only not half-men, but that they are perfectly normal mothers. Whether or not people think lesbians ought to be mothers is not really a point to be argued; there are already thousands of them, all over the world, bringing up their children just like other mothers do. We want to introduce you to some of these mothers, their friends and their children, so that you can see for yourselves how normal and ordinary they are. Well, not quite ordinary, since they bear a heavier burden of nastiness from the rest of society than do most other people, and they need, therefore, more courage to live their lives. But normal, yes. They're as normal as anyone else is, having their fair share of domestic squabbling, pressures of work and money, anxieties about their children, and, sometimes, the pain of broken relationships. Lesbian mothers, in particular, are very concerned about the welfare of their children. During our research for this book, we did not come across, or hear about, one case of child-abuse, neglect or rejection. In cases where husbands have fought their lesbian wives for custody of the children, the mothers who lost their children – because the court assumed that a lesbian cannot be a proper mother – suffered the normal grief and despair that any normal mother would suffer when forced to give away her children.

In the summer of 1978 we set out on a tour of England and Wales to meet lesbian mothers and their families, to talk to them, to see how they lived and to give them a chance to speak in their own words to the public. They co-operated fully, with one reservation – that they must remain anonymous. We found that this request had nothing to do with doubts or shame or guilt about their personal lives. On the contrary, they were proud to have fought their private battles for the freedom to live and love in the way that most fulfils them. Not one of the women we met had been the victim of a 'lesbian attack'. Not one had been corrupted by an evil older woman. They had discovered, in ways which they will tell themselves, the beauty and mystery of being able to love a person of their own sex. Their fear of discovery, in every case, arose from their concern for their children. Like all mothers, they want, where they can, to protect their children from the viciousness of human nature. Knowing only too well themselves how exhausting and painful it is to carry, day in and day out, the stigma of social disapproval, they want their children to develop as other children do – getting on at school, making their own friends, enjoying their own interests. These mothers do not want their children to become objects of careless curiosity, pity or contempt. That is why the names in this book have been changed. That is why there are no photographs of family life – of christenings and holidays and parties, of children playing or of women being tender with each other and with their children.

It seems unfortunate that, in a liberal democracy, in the late twentieth century, so many harmless women and innocent children should have cause to be afraid.

We may not have photographs but we have the women's words. And the most encouraging thing is that the women have wanted to tell what they know and what they have experienced. One mother wrote to us, for example, 'Of course we as lesbians want children, naturally our children will be loved and normal, we are, after all, normal ourselves. I only wish others could understand the warmth, support, care, and love that is the strength of the lesbian movement.'

The mothers and families we met are living in a variety of very different circumstances. Some are still married, some are divorced or separated from their husbands, and some were never married. Some are living with a lesbian lover and children, whereas others are living alone with their children. Some are living in larger households which include other adults. Their jobs are as varied as their life-styles; they include full-time mothers, farmers, part-time students, nurses, journalists, teachers, a computer programmer, a photographer, a singer, a TV technician, a gardener, a civil servant, an architect, a waitress, a cashier and a cleaner. The oldest mother we met was in her mid-fifties; the youngest was twenty-three.

The number of children in the families ranged from one to four. Although several of the mothers had four children and still managed to support them, most had two children, and all the young mothers, whose single children were still toddlers, said they wanted two children. The ages of the children themselves ranged from one year to twenty-three; we were able, therefore, to ask the older children whether they had suffered from having a lesbian mother.

Apart from the different kinds of relationships in these families, there were also regional and class differences, and differences of race and religion. We visited every kind of dwelling, from council house to private estate, from temporary shack to country cottage. We met white women and black women, Catholic, Jewish, nonconformist and atheist. We heard views ranging from conservative to Marxist, from feminist to even anti-feminist. There were, in short, no ideas, circumstances, or experiences which all these women would have in common, except that they are mothers. And that they are all lesbians.

The methods used for our investigation were more those of the journalist than of the scientific researcher. Many of these women had already been subject either to formal questioning for the purposes of quantitative research, or to legal questioning, or to what some felt was highly aggressive questioning on behalf of the social services. Many resented that they had not been asked what they really wanted to tell or that what they had meant had been interpreted in misleading or inaccurate ways. Many were, anyway, anxious about exposure and ensuing prejudice.

We have not, therefore, chosen to match the sample, to use systematic techniques or to standardize a questionnaire. We chose, instead, to engage in open-ended conversations in the hope that the women's own points of view could most easily emerge.

Gillian E. Hanscombe
Jackie Forster

Acknowledgments

Our thanks, in the first instance, go to the women, men and children whose willingness to talk in public about their private lives has provided the impetus for and the direction of this book.

For expert and friendly advice, freely given, we thank Tony, David, Tom, Sue, Joan and Andrew.

For technical help with the manuscript, also freely given, we thank Zoe and Ann.

For information provided on request we thank Nancy Duiguid and Gay Sweatshop; the National Council for One-Parent Families; the Royal College of Obstetricians and Gynaecologists; National Gay Task Force (United States), who sent us material collated by them; and *Lesbian Connection* for putting us in touch with American lesbian mothers.

For their kind permission to quote from published works and articles, thanks are due to *Sappho* magazine for permission to reprint the story of Selina and Martha; the Royal College of Obstetricians and Gynaecologists for extracts from *Artificial Insemination,* Proceedings of the Fourth Study Group of the Royal College of Obstetricians and Gynaecologists, edited by Michael Brudenell, Anne McLaren, Roger Short and Malcolm Symonds; the National Council for One-Parent Families for extracts from 'One-Parent Families'; the Social Welfare Commission of the Catholic Bishops' Conference for extracts from *An Introduction to the Pastoral Care of Homosexual People*; Messrs Little, Brown & Co. Inc. for an extract from *Homosexuality in Perspective* by William H. Masters and Virginia E. Johnson; Messrs Pan Books Ltd for an extract from *One Parent Families* by Diana Davenport; and Messrs Quartet Books Ltd for an extract from *Deliver Us From Love* by Suzanne Brøgger, translated from the Danish by Thomas Teal.

Thanks, finally, to all our friends, for support, encouragement and hours of chat – and, too, the making of much coffee. . . . More people make a book than the authors.

G.E.H.
J.F.

Introduction

This book is essentially about lesbian mothers – their children, lovers, husbands, friends, families, and their opinions, experiences, hopes and fears. It is also about how to get pregnant, how to cope with the law, and how to live in new ways. But before meeting the lesbian women who speak in this book, it is necessary to know something about lesbian sexuality and to think very carefully indeed about love, sex, marriage and child-bearing, which are so often muddled up together but which are separate experiences with separate consequences.

In the first place, there are differences between male and female sexuality which arise from basic anatomy. In the case of the man, who ejaculates sperm every time he experiences orgasm, having sex and making babies are very much interconnected. In the case of the woman, on the other hand, having sex is mostly nothing to do with having babies, because her experience of orgasm is not connected at all with the presence or absence of an egg.

Secondly, the idea that sex is only natural when it results in making babies is one which would make hundreds of millions of sexual acts unnatural – masturbation, oral sex, anal sex, homosexual sex, heterosexual sex with contraception, heterosexual sex between infertile couples, heterosexual sex between old couples, and so on. By the same token, group sex resulting in pregnancy, rape resulting in pregnancy, and all forms of sexual abuse in which a woman is inseminated and becomes pregnant, would be called natural. To most people such possibilities are absurd. What is natural, more simply, is what *comes naturally*. Sexuality, in all its adult forms, is an important part of every human being's experience and it plays an essential part in the civilizing process of society.

Thirdly, the idea that the nuclear family is the best environment for bringing up children is a modern prejudice. The nuclear family is by no means universal and has a relatively short history. Indeed, it now seems to many people, including ourselves, that there are more things to be said against it than there are to be said for it. A closer look at some of these points in relation to lesbian women will show more clearly how lesbian motherhood can provide a guide to the direction our society may take in the future.

Lesbians, after all, are women. The body of a lesbian woman is no different from the body of a non-lesbian woman. Whether a woman is a lesbian or a non-lesbian, she shares with her sisters the same anatomy, the same chemistry, the same menstrual cycle and the same capacity for child-bearing. It is not possible, by looking at a group of women, to pick out the lesbian women among them simply by looking. A great deal of research has been done in the past to try to find out how lesbian women are different from non-lesbian women, but none we know of has found any significant differences. Lesbians do not even have more male hormones than other women. Lesbians are just women, not imitation men, or pseudo-men, or half-men.

Perhaps because researchers could not find any physical differences between lesbian and non-lesbian women, they turned to the idea that there must be psychological differences between these two groups of women. Lesbians must be women who specially hated their fathers, for example. Not so. It became clear that many of them did not hate their fathers, and indeed many of them hated their mothers. Most did not hate either their fathers or their mothers. The research continued. Lesbians must be women who hate men. But many of them have close relationships with fathers, brothers, bosses, friends and ex-. husbands. Many lesbians have close relationships with husbands to whom they are still married. And many have sons, whom they certainly do not hate at all. Indeed, lesbian feminists of the American Women's Movement, along with lesbian feminists in other countries, became lesbians purely for reasons of political principle – and even they found that they could transfer their sexuality from men to women quite easily. That is a piece of common knowledge. The transference of sexuality which takes place in single-sex schools, women's prisons and other places where women are kept together without men for a lengthy period of time, is another example of the fact that it is *human* sexuality which is natural, not merely the one particular form of heterosexuality. It is becoming more and more obvious that lesbian sexuality is a way of feeling and behaving that is dormant in every woman, that is open to all women, and that is only kept suppressed by social taboos and disapproval. Many of the lesbian women in this book, for example, only discovered their lesbian potential after years of marriage.

Most people would say that they don't know any lesbians. But estimates of the incidence of lesbianism vary between one in six and one in twenty of the adult female population, and since most people know between six and twenty adult women, it follows that most people will know at least one lesbian. It is not surprising that people are often so hostile and aggressive towards lesbians when lesbian women choose to keep their sexuality secret, even from their families and friends. It is much more surprising that the differences lesbian women are supposed to have, which are supposed to mark them off from 'normal', 'decent', 'feminine' women, are not obvious enough to be seen. The truth is that lesbian women are no more and no less normal than non-lesbian women and that is the real reason why people cannot spot lesbians in a group.

Like non-lesbian women, lesbians come in all shapes and varieties. Some are ambitious, others are not. Some are neurotic, others are not. Some are married, others are not. Some are clever, others are not. Some are mothers, others are not. Furthermore, out of all the *non-lesbian* women who are not mothers, there are many who would like to be. And similarly, out of all the *lesbian* women who are not mothers, there are many who would like to be. One of the cruel inefficiencies of our society is our obsession with what is called the 'normal' or 'nuclear' family – i.e., a man and a woman who are married to each other and who bring up their children together. Women are still taught that the best way in which they can, or should, become mothers, is to 'fall in love' with a man and then 'get married' to him. It is becoming more obvious, as our century wears on, that many women are refusing to comply with this teaching. The demand is too high. The demand is, quite simply, that women should be able to bring together their romantic feelings, their sexual needs, their maternal drives and their capacities for work. All in one place. All when they are young and inexperienced. And all for ever. To those women who do not 'fall in love' with a man, or who 'fall in love' with a man who can't or won't marry, or who 'fall in love' with a woman, or who do not 'fall in love' with anyone, society says 'tough luck'. Such women are made to feel that they have no right to have children. And strangely enough, after the event, most women will agree that 'falling in love' has nothing to do with being a mother. But that is after the event.

Like many non-lesbian women, some lesbians have wanted children so much that they have 'fallen in love' with men, have 'got married' and have become mothers. That is not really surprising when it has been, for so long, the only acceptable way to have children. And it is not surprising for another reason as well – most lesbians, like most non-lesbians, do not hate men. What is special about lesbians is that they are able to love women. Why lesbians should be despised, ridiculed and rejected for being able to love women is indeed puzzling and the subject for many as yet unwritten books. In spite of this, they go on loving women. And also in spite of this, many of them are mothers.

A huge burden of public ignorance has been created by society's obsession with the nuclear family, which is assumed to be an ideal environment for the working out of ideal relationships between women and men and their children. But this nuclear family excludes all sexual love-relationships except married heterosexual monogamy. The fact that this exclusion has caused unspeakable problems for so many people must make us wonder, seriously, whether the reasons why society persists with the nuclear family are that it serves the economic and other interests of the State and of the entrenched religions. For many, many people the 'normal' family does not offer any chance for personal liberation.

A special problem for women (when they are allowed to say that it is a problem – and when anyone is willing and able to listen to them) is the double role of wife and mother. Women are somehow expected to fuse together their sexual feelings and their maternal feelings. Many, even most, married women are forced, over and over again, to choose between the welfare of their husbands and the welfare of their children. A woman can't be two people at once. But she is expected to be. It is essential to understand how separate a woman's sexual feelings really are from her maternal feelings. And this division can only be understood if it is clear, at the beginning, that there are important differences between a man's sexuality and a woman's sexuality.

The widespread use of the pill and other modern contraceptives has shown beyond doubt that women are eager and willing to experience sexual pleasure entirely for its own sake. In such a situation, having a baby is absolutely irrelevant, because the woman has made the choice between becoming pregnant and not becoming pregnant. Nevertheless, she still wants sex. We can see from this what we may always have suspected but were never able to prove before – that women like sex for its own sake, not because they want to have babies. Before modern contraception, lesbian sex was one of the forms of feminine sexuality which showed this fact. In spite of this, we were taught, mainly by religion, that the only 'natural' reason for human sexuality existing at all was the reproduction of the species. Because of this doctrine, lesbian sexuality, like heterosexuality with contraception, was called a perversion of nature. Once it is clear that people only *sometimes* have sex in order to make babies, but at all other times have sex *without* wanting babies, it is very hard to see why there should be any objection to lesbian sexuality. It is much more reasonable, and much more obvious, to see that for women sexual pleasure is one thing, and the reproduction of the species is another. These two things may, of course, occur together, but they *need not*. For men, on the other hand, the opposite is true; biologically, sexual pleasure and the reproduction of the species *must* occur together. We can understand this by looking carefully at the male and female sexual parts and their functions.

Research by the American scientists Masters and Johnson showed that the female orgasm is definitely located in the complex of nerve-endings in the clitoris. (The human female is unique among primates in having an orgasm at all.) Masters and Johnson showed also, however, that women, unlike men, not only have orgasm, but are capable of multiple orgasm. This means that with proper stimulation of the clitoris, either direct or indirect, any woman who is physically healthy and who does not suffer psychological inhibitions, will experience one or more orgasms. Whether or not she has a penis (or anything else) in her vagina at the time, stimulation of the clitoris will result in the same physical experience of orgasm. Some women will prefer orgasm with penetration, some without penetration, and some will not mind either way. That is a matter of taste and feeling. But there can be no doubt that the clitoris is the woman's sexual organ.

The human embryo in the womb does not become differentiated into one sex or the other until roughly six weeks have passed. It is also known that the clitoris and the penis develop from exactly the same sex-cells. Both the clitoris and the penis are capable of orgasm. What is different, though, is that the penis, in addition to its sexual function of orgasm, also has a reproductive function – the ejaculation of sperms in order to fertilize an egg and begin a baby. When a man has an orgasm, he ejaculates sperms. Unless he is diseased, he cannot have the one without the other. Every single time he has the sexual pleasure of orgasm, he is in the position of potentially fathering a child. The clitoris, however, has nothing to do with making babies – its sole function is to produce sexual pleasure. The *reproductive* system of the woman is the complex of ovary, womb and vagina. The vagina is especially important because it both receives the sperms and guides the new baby out into the world. A woman's vagina may certainly produce pleasurable sensations, but it is physically much less sensitive than the clitoris. The woman has two differentiated systems in her body – she has a sexual-arousal system and she has a reproductive system. *And one may be activated independently from the other.* That is *not* the case for the man.

Another way of getting this clear is to think of the possible ways men and women have sex, on the one hand, and make babies, on the other. We know from ordinary experience, for example, that it is possible to (a) stimulate a woman to orgasm without penetration of the vagina; and (b) inseminate a woman through male orgasm and ejaculation whether or not she has experienced sexual pleasure.

With (a) we can include all instances of female masturbation without the use of a penis or penis-substitute, all instances of lesbian love-making without penetration, and all instances of heterosexual love-making except vaginal penetration. With (b) the most obvious case is that of rape, where a man can achieve an orgasm and make a woman pregnant, even though the experience gives her no sexual pleasure at all and can even cause her great pain.

When we think in the same way about men, it is clear that they cannot (a) be stimulated to orgasm without the ejaculation of sperms; or (b) inseminate a woman without experiencing orgasm.

These are natural, or biological, facts, and they mean that an act of sexual pleasure for a man is always an act of potential fathering, but for a woman an act of sexual pleasure is not necessarily an act of potential mothering. They also mean that it is possible for a woman to become a mother without any sexual pleasure at all. The sexual arousal system of the woman is actually not necessary for maternity at all.

As well as these differences in anatomy, there are also psychological differences between women and men. Developmental theories, such as Freud's, make a strong point of the boy infant's dependence on his mother and the part it plays in establishing his male gender identity. But the girl infant is equally dependent on her mother. If a boy 'falls in love' with his mother, as Freud suggested, so too must the girl. The complication to this theory, worked out by Freud and others, is that the girl (but not the boy) must also, at some later stage, 'fall in love' with her father, so that she will be able to make heterosexual relationships when she is adult. That may or may not be true; what is important for our purposes is that a girl, like a boy, learns her first and basic experiences of love from her mother. This suggests that the search for *relationship* (not just for a body) is deeply rooted in a person's original need for the love and care provided by his or her mother. In the case of the male, he has no need to change his intuitive response, because the object of his need, love and desire is already female, like his mother. In the case of the female, on the other hand, she will either seek someone who is already female, like her mother, or she will somehow have to 'feminize' a male – make him more emotionally recognizable – so that she can embrace him in a love-relationship. Women want relationships – they don't want just sex. Women are, in this way, emotionally bisexual; they can 'fall in love' with women and with men. With women because of their identification with their own mothers and with men because, as mothers, they give birth to men as well as to women. In fact, they often 'mother' their male partners as much as they mother their own children.

Women can get sexual pleasure from either women or men, because stimulation of the clitoris can be offered by either sex. The act of vaginal penetration by the penis is not necessary for female orgasm, even though many women may prefer it for psychological reasons. It is equally true that the man has no need of the vagina for his orgasm. Obviously all the sexual behaviours which give pleasure to women and men must be natural, simply because the experiences of love, of sexuality and of making babies, are different experiences. The only case in which there is a biological reason for vaginal penetration by a penis is the case in which a baby is going to be made. It is rather silly to generalize from that one case – how babies are made – to all other kinds of sexuality in order to argue that other kinds of sexuality are unnatural because they don't make babies. They are not *supposed* to make babies.

A part of the body does not necessarily have only *one* natural function. For example, what would be the natural function of the mouth? Eating? Talking? Kissing? Breathing? A human mouth can do all these things, but surely no one of them is more natural than the others. As for a human hand, it can do many hundreds of different things, all of them as natural as each other. The attempt to make people think that sexual pleasure and making babies are the same thing has worked for a long time, but we are now in a position to re-examine that idea and to see how much of women's experiences it leaves out.

There is one final point. Women and men give an equal half of the material of a new human being because they give one reproductive cell each. Up to the point of fertilization they are equal partners in the reproductive process. In the creative process, however, men play no part at all. It is within a woman's body that a new baby must grow from the fertilized cell. Not only does the womb provide space and nourishment for the growing foetus, but every system in the mother's body is radically altered in order to sustain the new life. The nine months' pre-natal environment of the womb provides the first non-genetic influences on the personality of the new human being. In addition, only women know that the children they bear are their own, whereas men can never really be sure. Before a baby is born the mother's part is already considerably greater than the father's.

Two important general areas need to be remembered, then, when we look at motherhood from the point of view of the woman. The first is the separate sexual arousal system which women have, and the second is the more intense investment which a woman makes in her parenthood. It is understandable that these things could present considerable psychological threat to men, who have, on the whole, been educated into a sense of superiority which is a feature of the sort of patriarchal society in which we live. It is not women's fault that men suffer this threat – it is the fault of patriarchy, which has for many centuries misunderstood both the nature and the purpose of female sexuality. We do not intend, in this book, to suggest that men are inferior or irrelevant, but we do suggest that the very existence of lesbian mothers shows clearly that motherhood is a peculiarly female phenomenon which has no natural dependence on a heterosexual life-style. The children of lesbian mothers are living proof of this; they have been for centuries and will continue to be. The idea that these children suffer special psychological damage is at present a common prejudice, not supported by any scientific evidence that we know of. The children themselves do not exhibit any unusual characteristics, as we hope will become obvious through the pages of this book.

It may take a long time before the ideas we have been considering are fully understood, especially when so many people are still unaware that they have lesbian women among their friends and families. We hope, as the prejudices die away, that lesbians and lesbian mothers will eventually be able to speak to the public face to face, without fear of being mocked or pitied or discriminated against. But unfortunately, it seems to us, that time is still in the future.

1 The Getting of the Children

It seemed to us that the first question most people might ask a lesbian mother would be how she came to be a mother at all. Apart from thinking that a lesbian is the strange half-man we described earlier, people also often believe that a lesbian is unable to endure heterosexual intercourse, let alone choose it or even enjoy it. It is therefore supposed, quite mistakenly, that lesbian women never marry; either because they are so ugly that no man would ever wish to marry them, or because they would never be able to perform wifely duties, or because they hate men so much that they would never have anything to do with them. We found the opposite to be the case; all the mothers we met, even those who had subsequently conceived children by artificial insemination, had had sexual contact with men; and in the older age groups all of them were, or had been, married. In addition, nearly all of the lesbian lovers we met had also had sexual contact with men. The overwhelming impression we got from all our conversations with the women was not that they fiercely hated men, but that they fiercely loved women. A point that Dr Charlotte Wolff makes in her study *Love Between Women* was reinforced in our minds – lesbians are not women who reject men, but women who choose women, because they enjoy them more. When there was hatred or resentment against men, it arose from two sources : either because a husband had maliciously contested, and won, a custody case, so that the mother had lost her children as a direct result of being a lesbian – or because of a radical feminist outlook, which had elicited hostility from men. It was hard for us to get any male responses to the idea of lesbian motherhood, because most of the husbands and fathers refused to talk to us or to offer their opinions. We have regretted not having more of the men's views, but we could

21

do no more than ask. In many instances, therefore, we must report what the mothers have said about the attitudes of the fathers of their children. Perhaps at a later date, some of these men might feel able to contribute.

We begin with Angela, who had one of the most unusual conceptions of all. Angela lives with her four children in a comfortable detached house on a new estate in the Home Counties. She works in one of the 'helping professions', is a practising Catholic, a contented mother and an articulate woman. When we asked her about the conception of her first child, she told us the following remarkable story :

'I was physically attracted to quite a few men, but I didn't want to have sex with them. . . . I decided I needed to go out with someone who was lighthearted, so I then went out with my husband, and I had petting sessions with him. I didn't know what happened with men, how the sperm got there and where they came from, or that it had anything to do with men having an orgasm. I became pregnant, though physically I was a virgin.

'If you masturbate a man so that he has an orgasm, and as long as you don't have any clothing covering the vagina and the sperms fall in the area of the vagina and there's plenty of liquid around, they can get into the vagina and you can still have your hymen intact. I hadn't been penetrated at all.

'I was twenty-one. When I didn't have my periods for three months I didn't believe I was pregnant. Eventually I went to a doctor, and he gave me some iron tablets – to pick me up ! I did have morning sickness. I told my mother. She said the best thing I could do was to go away to a home and have it adopted straight away. She said, "Do you want to get married?" When faced with those two alternatives I chose marriage. He offered to marry me out of politeness. I chose to ignore that fact. I wanted the baby. I always wanted children very much. I always imagined myself as a mother and I did feel this would make me belong to the set of heterosexual people.'

Penny, on the other hand, didn't have such an easy time of it. When we went to visit her, she introduced us proudly to her two children, Jean, aged twelve, and Michael, aged sixteen, and said all that she had to say with both of them present. It was a happy, relaxed atmosphere, full of warmth, teasing and affection. Clearly Penny had nothing to hide from her children and they, in their turn, showed how fond they were of her. They live in a semi-detached house in a London suburb, quite unlike Angela's orderly house – the children's records and magazines were scattered about and Penny brought beer and sandwiches for us all, which we spread on the carpet. She told us that she had already been through lesbian experiences before she met her husband-to-be. 'He was older than me,' she explained, 'about thirty-three or four. I was just over sixteen.' What attracted her was that he 'wasn't a sexual type. He didn't make advances.' He wanted to marry her and, because he had treated her well, she agreed. When we asked her if she had been in love with him, she said no, but she had liked him and that after her stormy lesbian affairs it was 'peaceful'. But as the reality of the wedding approached, she began to get nervous :

'I'd never had sex with a man. I did wonder what it was like. It was in August. I had a lot to drink; I'm not using drink as an excuse, because you still know what you're doing. Anyway, it happened but I didn't like it. It hurt. Nothing happened, but I did miss my period. I think it was a psychological thing.

'Then I got cold feet. The banns were being arranged. My father was up in arms about it; he said, "You're seventeen, he's not for you – I don't like it." He was still trying to talk me out of it on the way round to the church, with the bouquet held upside down. I got married in September. We went away on a honeymoon, which wasn't one. He got drunk all the time.

'There was something wrong, somewhere,' Penny concluded. Then she added, 'I only slept with him thirty times.' Surprised, we asked if she had counted. 'Yes,' she replied, 'it was so horrible. It really was.' Had her husband been at all sympathetic to her reactions? She replied that he had said she wasn't normal and had made 'general nasty remarks'.

Unlike Angela, when Penny suspected she might be pregnant, she was horrified. 'I couldn't picture myself as a mother. I've always loved kids. That's nice for other women, but I couldn't picture myself with a pram, a baby. It made me feel trapped in marriage. . . . I was in a trauma. I couldn't believe it was happening to me. When I decided I'd give marriage twelve months and it would all come to an end, and that the baby was part of him,

I decided it would have to be adopted. I didn't want to see it. I didn't want any part of it. My sister, who's very straight and very maternal, said she'd have it.'

We asked if she had considered an abortion. 'Yes,' she said, 'but it wasn't legal then.' In addition, Penny had an uncomfortable pregnancy: 'I was very sick, every, every morning.' But when Penny's baby son was finally born, she describes her first reaction as the state of being 'transformed'. All her feelings of rejection vanished:

'I'd been in pain for such a long time, and all these plans – give it up, get rid of it – then when you see it, it's the most marvellous feeling. It's a miracle. I think every birth is a miracle.

'They held him up. They cut the cord. I had to have stitches, twenty-one stitches. They weighed the baby: I was expecting a freak. They said, "You've a beautiful baby boy." I was on the stretcher, the baby was bathed and placed in his cot near me. If somebody had walked in and offered me a million pounds, the answer would have been "No." He was marvellous.'

We asked Penny whether she had wanted a second baby. 'Oh no,' she said. Had she been using contraception then? 'Oh no,' she said again. Then she explained: 'Well, nothing was going on. I was staying with my husband's brother and his wife, because she wanted to meet me. I stayed there a year.' Then her husband came on visit and she had sex with him. It was the last time.

Rachel, unlike both Angela and Penny, was never married. When we asked how she had become pregnant and how she had dealt with the pregnancy, she told us: 'I had a relationship with a man. I wasn't married. We had something going. He lived abroad, I lived in England. We had our own lives and we would meet from time to time. We were together, really. I always wanted to establish my independence from him . . . I mean live separately and together. I just got pregnant. I wanted a child. I hadn't planned it, I sort of let myself get pregnant. I stopped taking the pill for a week, thinking I wouldn't get pregnant, being on it for so many years. It was a real shock. I hadn't even thought of it right then. I immediately thought of an abortion. I had very little money and was living in a squat in the East End. It seemed impossible. So I went along to this supposedly sympathetic GP. He told me there was a waiting list. I think I was about seven weeks pregnant then. He said I would have to wait for a month to six weeks on the National Health Service. It was to be a twelve-week abortion.

'There are long waiting lists in hospitals. Most women go and get private abortions. So I booked for an abortion. As time went by, I started to think, "Well, I'm twenty-six." My mother was living with me and she was encouraging me to have an abortion. I kept weighing it up in my mind the whole time – "How will I ever get pregnant again?" It was agonizing, those weeks, really agonizing. All the time at night, I'd just lie there, really dying to have the baby; it just seemed impossible. Eventually it was June '76. It was a beautiful summer that summer. I was supposed to go into hospital at three o'clock in the afternoon and I still hadn't decided. It was this beautiful day. I woke up in the morning and I walked around all day, went to see my friends and I came back home. I just never went to the hospital. My mother looked at me, she nearly died. She was quite shocked. I had a lot of friends in the squat and other friends, some of them were mums. Everybody knew it was my decision, but I was getting a lot of support about the pros of having a child. I didn't discuss it much with the father. He did say, "Fine, if you have the baby, it's fine by me." He was always coming and going. He never had any money. He was a pretty unstable sort of character. I couldn't rely on him. I knew it was my decision.'

We asked Rachel whether, after the birth of her son, she had wanted to get married. 'No,' she replied, 'I was quite decided about that.' What about the father? Did he want to marry her? 'Afterwards, he did. But not because of the baby. . . . After the baby was born, the father came back and he's very dependent on me, both emotionally and financially – and I told him about my lover. He went mad. It was like I was having this wonderful lesbian relationship behind his back, and he'd come back to see his baby. We had been writing to each other, so he went mad and he was going to kill her (she was sleeping upstairs).' He didn't kill Rachel's lover, nor did he try to take the baby away. He comes to visit from time to time and knows that Rachel has decided to bring up their son in a lesbian household in which the other women share responsibility for the child.

Pat, also unmarried, works in the entertainment business. When we went to visit her London flat, we were introduced to her lover, Sally, and her two sons, Tom and Terry. Terry is only three and soon went to bed, but Tom, aged thirteen, stayed with us, heard all that was said, and occasionally joined in the conversation.

Pat explained that she had had a lesbian relationship at the age of sixteen, when she was a 'teeny' pop-singer. Later, at nineteen, she 'started to get the itch' that she hadn't had any childhood and hadn't even been to dances. She thought, in her words, 'P'raps I was heterosexual and didn't know. I met Tom's father at P. J. Proby's party. I got engaged to him – he was "it" in the business.' When we pressed her on why she chose him rather than anyone else, she responded immediately, 'My mother would have approved!' That was important to her, because she felt nobody had approved of anything she had done up till then. There was going to be a 'big posh wedding', until she discovered she was pregnant.

We asked if she had been in love with her husband-to-be. 'I was in love with the idea of doing it all properly,' she replied. 'I wasn't thinking. I was being totally ridiculous. He was infatuated with me. He was quite nice. . . . I can't really say I've been in love with a man at all. I can't honestly say it was a relationship. It was something I was doing because it was expected of me, and I'd been conditioned to do it.'

The pregnancy, however, changed Pat's plans: 'As soon as I found out I was pregnant, I decided there was no point in getting married. I've never been a promiscuous sort of person. I tend to do things socially the right way round. My own sense told me, "This is what I want – to be pregnant – let's get rid of the other fripperies and sort myself out." I went back to my girl-friend.' Had Tom's father wanted to see the baby? 'We discussed it. He was a very stable person – he knew about my relationship – and said, "Well, I suppose you'll be going back?" Which I did. He was absolutely British about the whole thing. I bumped into him once, in Portobello Road. He asked if I needed anything and gave me his card. Very nice chap.'

With a ten-year gap between Pat's two sons, we wondered how she had come to have a second child. She explained: 'Tom was always going on about wanting a brother, which I decided was the best excuse for having one. I was so happy while pregnant, and the first few years with Tom were blissful. I did the full mum. It knocked me out, everything about it. . . . Around this time I was breaking up with my girl-friend. I thought I was quite happy with the situation. I told myself I was. Obviously I wasn't. So to cheer myself up I went and got pregnant. I was away doing cabaret. I saw this likely-looking chappie. It worked. It was a one-off. I knew there was a four-day period. I had a feeling that that day was the one. I was right.'

Pat is thirty-four. The straightforward deliberation she expressed about wanting to be pregnant was even more marked, we found, among the younger women. Anne and Liz, for example, planned both their two children; even though Anne is the mother, both women feel the children belong to them equally, since they planned them together and are living as a family. They have a small country cottage with a vegetable garden; Anne stays at home with the children while Liz goes to work in a local hospital. We asked how they had come to have children and Anne explained that at the time of planning the first, they were not actually living together. They had, nevertheless, had a relationship for a long time and had discussed having a baby 'for years previously'. They chose as the father a 'mutual friend' who had been at the same college as Liz. Because Anne had a nursing background, she knew how to take her own temperature to make a chart of her ovulation cycle so that she could calculate precisely when she would be fertile. She began having sexual intercourse with the mutual friend one February, during her fertile days, and repeated the act each month until June, when she became pregnant. We asked whether having sex with a man for these four months had caused her any stress or anxiety, to which she replied, 'I just wanted a baby. I was quite fond of him really.'

For the second child, they did not choose the same father. 'He had set up home with another woman and he was involved. Our friendship had drifted since he left college. We decided that perhaps it wasn't fair,' Liz explained, and Anne added, 'We decided that we couldn't bear the hassle.' The hassle involved planning meetings away from home, as Anne elaborated for us: 'I had

had to plan in advance because I was at college. It just happened that it had been the holidays. Twice I stayed with him at the beginning of the holidays and at the end. I didn't become pregnant. He'd gone off to Greece. It just happened that I had gone to London for an interview for a job. It just happened that he came back from Greece and came to see me and stayed the night.'

We asked Liz whether she hadn't been afraid that Anne might form a relationship with this man, to which she answered, 'Some anxiousness is natural, isn't it? Possibly not more than I would, you know, feel that there was a possibility she would find somebody else.' We also asked whether, after the birth of Anne's baby, the father hadn't wanted to see him. 'It's not his son !' said Anne immediately, and then added that she had told him the baby had been born but that he 'wasn't very interested', probably, she thought, 'because he was very heavily involved with this woman' (with whom he had set up house).

For their second child Anne and Liz decided to use artificial insemination. The doctor suggested that they should ask the first child's father whether he would be willing to be the donor for the second, which Anne and Liz hadn't thought of. They wrote to him but he said no. They went ahead, therefore, with artificial insemination from an unknown donor, under the direction of the doctor. Despite their nursing background, they hadn't thought of artificial insemination the first time because they had never heard of it being used without the prospective mother having a husband (i.e. as therapy for an infertile marriage). But once they heard that lesbian women were receiving artificial insemination in order to conceive children, they went to a doctor who was willing to help them. This time Anne conceived more quickly, having only two inseminations during one fertile period, and her second baby, a daughter, was born without any problems.

Kath and Vera, who are in their mid-twenties, wanted very much to have children. Of all the women we met, Kath and Vera showed perhaps the most persistence in their quest for a child. They live in a remote part of England where they enjoy an idyllic natural environment and the advantages of village life. However, rural communities are very conservative and Kath and

Vera could not expect to find much local support or facilities for their plan to have a baby. Nevertheless it was clear between them that they wanted a child and that Kath would be the mother.

'I always wanted to have a child,' she told us. 'We talked about it. Vera didn't like the idea of bearing children. It's perfect, really, because Vera wanted a child without having to bear it. So we agreed very easily.' Vera added, 'We thought about how we were going to do it,' and Kath broke in, 'We thought about all the men we knew . . .' to be elaborated again by Vera, 'There weren't that many. . . .' Throughout the conversation Kath and Vera supported each other, spoke for each other, showed that they knew each other's thoughts and reactions intimately.

Kath explained that they decided that they didn't want to 'involve anyone in the area', so they then thought about AID, which they'd heard about through a lesbian organization. They telephoned one of the doctors whom they had been told would give AID to lesbians and he told them to begin taking a temperature chart. He explained to them how to do it and said he would like them to keep the chart going for two to three months. 'We kept so many charts,' said Vera with a laugh, 'about eight.' Kath's periods, it turned out, were very irregular. Then they went to London to see the doctor and the visit coincided roughly with Kath's ovulation. It was a bit early, but they thought they'd try an insemination, just in case they were lucky. It was a long and expensive train journey so they wanted to make as much use of their time in London as they could.

We shall discuss artificial insemination in detail in a later chapter; here we just want to explain briefly that the mother-to-be should have the insemination during her fertile days of the month and that when she is ready, semen is introduced into her vagina by using an ordinary syringe. The syringe does not need to have a needle attached to it, so there is nothing painful at all about the procedure.

Kath and Vera made an appointment with the doctor and went for a consultation. Kath explained what happened: 'He asked me why I wanted a child. Did we feel really responsible? He then said, "I can't make decisions for you, but if you've thought about it then that's your decision." He knew we were lesbians. He asked me about role-playing – why one of us wanted the child, which one of us was the femme. We said it was nothing like that. He looked at us and said, "OK, brown eyes, brown hair," and checked us for the characteristics. He gave me an internal examination. Then he talked about the temperature charts. He told us the procedure. That he thought it would be better if we did the insemination together. He showed us how to use the syringe.'

Vera : 'He showed me a needle and said, "You don't have to use this!" I hate needles, anyway. He showed me how to put the syringe into a small bottle where the semen would be and to draw it out with the syringe. He said Kath should lie there for about twenty minutes afterwards.'

Kath : 'He told me to relax. If we had intercourse, it would help make me less tense. That's why it would be better if Vera did it and not him. That was about it, and we arranged to go back the next day. When we arrived, the receptionist showed us into this little room. There was a couch.'

We asked if they had made love and if they thought it had helped, since the doctor had advised them that it would. They both replied that they 'couldn't have done it' but that they thought it might have helped if they had. 'The ideal thing,' Kath added, 'would have been to do it at home. Anyway, I lay there with my hips raised on telephone directories! A bit unnatural – not easy to make love like that!' And Vera, for her part, was equally unrelaxed : 'I was terrified. There was a very tiny amount of semen in the bottle. I was surprised at the small amount there was. Then we had to catch the train home. We arranged to go down the next month, for one day on a day-return. We couldn't afford to stay longer.' They did so, but there was a slight mishap the next time – Vera spilt some of the semen! She explained that the syringe had made her nervous.

They went home rather unhopeful and thinking that they would have to find something closer to home, since the journeys to London were so expensive. They got in touch with a gay social worker and wrote to the local hospitals trying to find out if there was any insemination service in their area. They had only one reply, and that was from a hospital which simply said 'No'. This approach was obviously leading nowhere. Next, Kath said, they decided to try gay men. 'That came to nothing,' Vera continued. 'I kept phoning – making all the calls. We couldn't afford to go to London again. Kath wasn't pregnant and we spent all summer following leads.' 'Everyone was sympathetic,' Kath added, 'but very frightened. Doctors, social workers, GLF [Gay Liberation Front]. We felt very low. It was very depressing. So we advertised in *Gay News* – "Two women interested in having a child." We got a lot of replies.' 'People wrote from everywhere,' said Vera. 'I phoned up one guy who was near. We arranged to meet. He was so lonely, it was obvious he just wanted to meet someone. I explained we just wanted a donor. He didn't think it was about AID. So nothing happened. I explained I was acting on behalf of two women – so I could get out of it.'

Kath went on : 'We had thought it out and picked up the tips from the London doctor. If we found a gay guy, we would drive him here, ask him to stimulate himself and ejaculate into a sterilized container. We had brought the syringe with us from London and we would insert it. Then we thought it would be better if the man left the semen at a friend's house, because it wasn't very wise to bring him here. We made all the arrangements with this other man who had answered our *Gay News* advertisement. Vera explained everything to him and offered to pay his travel expenses and meet him at the station. He was terribly nervous. So was Vera, but she tried to sound very off-hand in the station buffet ! She pretended she was a nurse and explained it all quite coldly. He said he understood. Because I was still reading the temperature chart, Vera said she would contact him in three weeks, when my temperature would go up.

'In the intervening weeks, we thought about meeting a man who was a virtual stranger. We thought there might be many lonely men who would like to meet a woman and the best thing to do would be to advertise in the local paper's personal columns. We felt terrible about this, actually, but we knew so few men amongst our acquaintances and we thought it better to meet someone we didn't know. Anyway, we did it. "Attractive single girl, twenties, seeks a guy for future companionship." We were inundated with replies. But before we put the ad in (we were quite hard-up at the time) we answered an ad in the paper already – "Businessman, twenty-five, seeks female." On the Thursday before the ad went in on Friday, he phoned me to go out with him. It seemed incredibly loose to go out for a few hours with this man, and then go back to his flat.' We wondered what this man was like. 'Just ordinary,' said Kath. 'A terrible egotist. He talked constantly about himself. He was twenty-five. He was healthy-looking. I didn't feel awful about using him; he had no hesitations about using me. I met him Friday night, and went to bed with him that night.'

We asked how Kath had felt and how she had coped with her feelings of anxiety or dislike. She had a novel answer : 'I was somebody else all the time. I didn't give my proper name. When he phoned up, I used another name. I created a character. I was divorced, with a past full of lovers. I quite enjoyed playing an act. . . . I didn't find him attractive. We didn't use any contraceptives. I was quite cold about the sex. I was untouched by it. It was just straight sex. He was quite persistent, which was all to the good; he had more than one ejaculation. He drove me home at about four in the morning. I told him I was only stay-ing here with friends.' At this point Vera added, 'I was some-body else, too.' 'So we arranged to go out on Sunday night,' Kath went on. We asked why. Wouldn't the next night have been better? Vera explained : 'Because Sunday was the nineteenth day, Kath, don't you remember? We thought it was too late. But we thought you should leave one day, and then do it again on the Sunday just to cover the ovulation, as the doctor had told us.' 'Yes, that was it,' Kath agreed. 'We were following the doctor's advice. Anyway, I went out with him on the Sunday and had sex. I told him I wanted to have a child and suggested we went away the next weekend. I think that shocked him. He wasn't sure he could make it because of business !'

'In the meantime,' Vera continued, 'we received all these replies to our ad in the local paper. We picked out three.' Kath was unaware that she might be pregnant. 'I chose one letter,' she said, 'from a musician – I met him. He was very, very nice and I wanted to keep him in tow. I was pessimistic about getting pregnant. I hadn't had any body changes. We went out twice but we didn't have any sex.' After two weeks, the businessman telephoned again. They told him that Kath had gone away, because they knew by now that she was pregnant. She had missed her period and had gone to the doctor for a pregnancy test. The test was positive. 'The business guy had worked,' said Kath. 'Katy is his daughter. We wound up all the letters. I wrote to the musician and told him I was pregnant!'

We have spent some time telling the story of how Kath became pregnant because it shows such a lot of planning and a very high degree of motivation. Whatever people might think about what Kath and Vera did, and however much they might disagree about the methods they tried, nobody could argue that Katy wasn't very much a wanted child.

It was this very strong desire of many lesbians to have children which most impressed a gynaecologist who went to one of their meetings. He had been asked by two lesbian women, who had been living together for some time, for artificial insemination. He confessed that he had never before been asked by lesbians for an insemination and he wanted to find out more about lesbians, their views and their reasons for having children. He thought it might clear his mind and help him to decide whether or not to give them what they wanted. He described his reactions to the meeting:

'There must have been about eighty people there – all women. I was the only male. Interestingly enough I didn't feel out of place. It wasn't as though I was a single man among women. It was a meeting of ordinary people. Nobody stared at me. I didn't feel I was in a place that was strange. That impressed me immediately. It was just a normal gathering of people. They divided up into three groups. One dealt with AID, another with children by heterosexual married contact and the other was adoption. Then we had the discussion in the little groups. The chairman of my group was one of the couple. Then there was the discussion afterwards. What I learnt on that day was that they were perfectly normal people, except in respect of their sexual relationship with their partner; that was the only difference I could detect – every other way they were perfectly normal.

'Another thing that impressed me was that someone said they had gone into a married situation just because they wanted children. A number of marriages had ended in divorce and they had taken their children and had gone to live with another woman after a lot of difficulty; a number said they had gone to street corners, pubs, that sort of thing, to try and get pregnant; they found that very distasteful, very unpleasant, they got very annoyed that they should have to depend on men at all. One person got up and said, "Why do we depend on men at all? We should pursue this idea of cloning." What came out of all this, to my mind, was that they very much wanted children and adoption was completely closed to them. That came out as well. I had never before had an opportunity to get a first-hand idea of what was behind this particular couple and other lesbians who wanted to have AID. I was very impressed. I suggested at that meeting that they didn't really need a doctor. What they needed was somebody to do the sort of work that an adoption society secretary would do, or a social worker, to put the people together. Basically, I think, a doctor's only required to vet the donor.'

The lesbian meeting which this gynaecologist attended reassured him that lesbians were 'perfectly normal', to use his own words, and that many of them were highly motivated to have children. Before that, he had never even thought about the subject. We asked him whether he had been outraged when the first lesbians he had known came to him wanting to be mothers. 'Not really,' he replied. 'I was taken aback, because I'd never been confronted by them. I'd never considered the situation. I'd never thought about it. As a doctor, I should have had far more knowledge about lesbians than the average lay person. Yet I had a complete blank as a gynaecologist in never having knowingly treated a lesbian. Yet this is not surprising when I met that roomful of perfectly normal women.'

When more lesbians came to him asking for inseminations, he decided that, because they were determined to have children anyway, and because he could not find anything about them which would make them worse mothers than non-lesbians, it would be preferable for them to have healthy men fathering their children than for them to go looking for casual pick-ups or, worse, to get involved in a marriage simply in order to have children.

The women who talked to us became pregnant in two broadly different ways: some got pregnant accidentally; the others set about it quite intentionally. These days, people tend to forgive women who get pregnant without meaning to – after all, it has been happening for hundreds of years. Many people even admire them for going on with the pregnancy and for devoting themselves to the bringing up of the child. But it is still a novel idea to think of women who are not married deliberately setting out to become pregnant. And the knowledge that they might 'use' men to get their children, without telling the men that the sole purpose is pregnancy, may seem rather shocking to some people. When we think about Pat, Anne and Kath, however, we should remember that in each case when the mother-to-be had heard of artificial insemination, she tried her best to use this method in preference to heterosexual intercourse. We have seen how this did not always work out. If Kath and Vera, for example, had not lived in a part of England in which the local hospitals and doctors were unhelpful, they would not have been forced to search for an unsuspecting father. Nevertheless, in the sense that they were not told why they were wanted, the fathers of these women's children were certainly 'used'.

With artificial insemination, the donor is fully aware that he is giving his semen in order to help a woman become pregnant. With Pat's second child, Anne's first child, and Kath's first child, the fathers did not know that these women were only having sex in order to get pregnant. In a way these men were cheated, much as married men are sometimes cheated by wives who desperately want children against the husband's will, and who say they have taken contraception when they haven't. All this means, of course, is that most women consider they have a right to bear children. When they find themselves in circumstances which seem to prevent their having children, and when all other avenues are closed, many of them are driven to use deceit. In this respect, some of our lesbian mothers do not seem to be much different from non-lesbian mothers; many women of each group will simply do whatever they have to in order to become pregnant. And unlike the 'cheating wife', the lesbian mother does not ask the father to take responsibility for the child.

We would suggest to men that if they seriously do not want to father children they must take responsibility for their own contraception, and not depend on women to do it for them. When men answer advertisements for a partner, or when they take women out with the intention of having sex with them, if they do not bother to find out whether or not a pregnancy might be the result, they can't expect much sympathy if later they claim to have been used.

At the 1979 annual conference of the British Medical Association it was decided that it should not be considered unethical for doctors to give artificial insemination to lesbians. As more and more doctors become involved in giving inseminations, less and less women will be forced into casual affairs or doomed marriages. They will be able to choose to have their children in an honest way. In the end, this will benefit men as well, in so far as they will be able to trust that the women with whom they have sexual relationships will want them for the sake of the relationship and not for possible pregnancies. Lesbians, like other women, want to be able to develop to the full the two sides of their feminine personality – their desire for a loving relationship and their desire for children.

2 Variations on a Theme

Are lesbian mothers 'proper' lesbians? Or are they really bi-sexuals? Or rebellious heterosexuals? These questions are based partly on the idea that 'real' lesbians are gruff-voiced, masculine creatures, and partly on an assumption that the maternal instinct and motherly feelings are somehow part and parcel of hetero-sexuality – that they 'just follow naturally' in the wake of mar-riage. The common idea is that women get married and have babies. Indeed, most of them still do, but there is evidence that this way of life is no longer as automatic as it once was, and it is certainly much less stable. It is becoming necessary, due to women's increasing control of their own fertility through con-traception and abortion, to look again at what feminine sexuality is really like and how much it is mixed up with having or not having children.

One academic gynaecologist we talked to agreed that it is becoming urgent for us all to think about the sorts of relation-ships we will be having in the future, when sexuality and child-bearing will become much more separated in people's minds than they are now. 'I think this is a very interesting area,' he said. 'Many gynaecologists still look a little strangely at the patient who has no children and comes in asking for sterilization. But then you're consulting men who think there's something important about producing babies. I can very well see that a lot of people would construe a pair of women wanting to live together and to have their own offspring as pathological. But then again for years and years people always called what upsets them, or what they can't come to a rational decision about, "pathological". I don't know that it necessarily is pathological.'

Lesbian mothers are an extremely good example of this dichot-omy between sexuality and child-bearing, because they develop

37

their need for a loving relationship in one area of their lives, but their desire for children in another. These areas may overlap, as in the case of married lesbians; or they may be separated, as in the case of lesbian women using artificial insemination. It is necessary, therefore, to look at how important their lesbian relationships have been for these mothers, and to see also whether they think their children have suffered in any way from their lesbianism.

Some of the women we met knew from early in their adolescence that they had the capacity to fall in love with people of the same sex. Angela dates her discovery of these feelings from the age of twelve. 'When it started,' she told us, 'I didn't know the word "lesbian", nor "gay". "Homosexual" was the one I knew, and that was only after I'd had a relationship. It didn't develop sexually – I was a bit backward. She [her friend] lent me a book.' Why had she done that? we asked. 'She tried to inform me in a gentle way,' Angela answered. How had Angela reacted to the book? 'I thought it was interesting,' she told us, 'because I could relate to it. There were school stories in my day where it was acceptable to have crushes, but they went through the phase into a heterosexual phase.' The book was called *A Bullet in the Ballet*; Angela explained that she could relate to the plot and setting because she was herself at a stage school and the person she was in love with was a ballet teacher. The relationship lasted for four years, 'with kisses and cuddles but no sex or orgasms'. They wrote a lot of letters to one another, which Angela's mother eventually found and read. Then Angela overheard her mother telling a relative that she'd discovered the letters. When her mother went out Angela looked in her mother's bedroom and found the letters in a drawer. She didn't understand what was wrong. 'I was completely innocent,' she explained, 'I had no feelings of guilt about it at all. Eventually I just sensed there was something dreadful about it. I took all the letters and burnt them. I wrote to the girl and told her. Again not even realizing what I was protecting. One of the letters asked me if I thought there was anything wrong in the relationship. She was merely talking about the fact that we were in love with each other. My mother naturally assumed that we were having a sexual relationship and started questioning me about what I'd done. I couldn't say anything other than I'd kissed her. She told me I was a liar and that I hadn't told her everything. But I had nothing to tell. She sat me down and kept questioning me. I was told I wasn't to see this girl any more. It was wrong. She then told me she'd had a crush on a girl, but it hadn't gone that far because she was terribly moral. Nothing had happened between her and this other girl. But it had obviously happened with me. I was disgusting and dirty. I had gone too far.

'I still went to the stage school. My friend said my mother had been over to the school and had threatened to get her dismissed unless she stopped seeing me. The head of the school was sympathetic towards both of us, but for the sake of the school itself she would have been prepared to sack her. I said I didn't know how to cope with this. My friend said, "Leave it for six months and see how you feel. And if you still can't cope, we'll think about it again." This gave me hope and kept me going on, really. I thought that was very sensible on her part. Because to cut me off completely – well, I would have fallen apart. I had other girl-friends at school and I palled up with one of them but I didn't feel the same way about her as I did about this other one. I knew nevertheless by that time there was something to be kept secret. I was reasonably happy with her [the second friend]. She had tendencies of epilepsy since a child and my mother told me off. She accused me of having brought the fits on because I put my arm around her. In fact I got quite worried that I might be making it worse.

'I was sixteen when the relationship was stopped,' she told us. 'My mother sent me to another school on the excuse I must study for O-levels and shouldn't be doing stage work. I was really upset. This girl's parents [the epileptic friend] arranged for me to meet the teacher I was in love with at their house. I kept wishing I had some physical illness – which I couldn't produce, no matter how hard I tried. Because it would have been far easier to cope with than having this emotional confusion. I had to keep going on, keep struggling and keep on living.'

We wondered how Angela's father had reacted to all this. He was somehow in the background, she explained. 'I couldn't go to him. Not that I didn't like him. I understood his values. He never spoke his affection, but I knew it was there. He never interfered with anything in the house. He was a pharmacist. And in those days they worked hard until 9 o'clock at night. I would see him hardly at all. I was busy doing this stage work and working till all hours of the night too. The stage school was also an agency and I was under contract to them. I was at an ordinary school during the day and would go on to the stage school in the evenings. I had to keep quiet about my age. We'd play nightclubs and dances. My mother came with me.'

The conversation turned back to Angela's mother. When she took Angela away from the stage school, she did not speak to her daughter for three months. At the end of this three months Angela was 'just about shattered'. She had managed to join an operatic society at which the teacher she was in love with was training the dancers for a production. Her mother didn't know about this, so she wasn't aware that Angela was seeing her friend once a week. But her mother had begun 'cutting down' all the things Angela liked: she had taken away her pocket money and other pleasures. Eventually Angela tried not to let her mother know that there was anything she liked, so that she couldn't take it away. But then 'she got to this one last thing, the operatic society, and said, "You're not going there any more." That was really it. I picked up a ballet shoe and threw it at the wall in temper. She hit me and broke my glasses and I walked out. I was going to leave home. I'd get as much money as I could find. I was going to get in touch with my epileptic friend's mother, hoping she'd put me up. Then I'd get a job.

'While I was out walking the streets, I thought about the things my mother had said to me. One was "I wish I had a lot more children and then I wouldn't give a damn about you. I'd just turn you out of the house and get rid of you. But because you're all I've got, you're the only one I can care about, do anything for." I was very sympathetic to my mother's problems. If I had walked out and never seen her again, the thought of her at home being sad about the fact that she'd made a mess of everything. . . .' So Angela returned home. Despite the hostility between them, mother and daughter still had need of each other's affection.

We asked Angela whether she had wanted boy-friends during this long period of her teenage years. 'I wanted to have boy-friends because everybody else had boy-friends,' she replied. 'I wanted to be the same as everybody else. I didn't like being kissed. I wanted to be thought attractive because I didn't think I was. Not that I was physically unattractive, but I didn't do anything to make boys attracted to me. The only males I was attracted to were married men, much older than myself.' In the end the pressures got too much for Angela. She felt that no one cared about her or noticed how unhappy she was. 'I used to go to exams with tears pouring down my face and nobody took a blind bit of notice. I was slumped over a desk in the lunch-hour and one person came up to me and asked, "Is there something wrong? Are you unwell?" I thought, "At last somebody has noticed!" So then I threw a fit. I copied what my epileptic friend did. They all came running round then. I was putting this on to attract attention in order to get some help. My father said to my mother, "Something's worrying her." The doctor gave me some barbiturates. By this time, I'd come to the conclusion that the relationship [with the ballet teacher] was not going to go on. I felt that she would get married, which she eventually did do. I saw her years later, after I was married, out of interest. I was really frightened. By that time, I thought I'd adjusted to being heterosexual. I thought I'd just go and see her and see how she was. I could feel that this attraction was still there. She asked me to help her get the washing in. It was pitch black night. I felt she was trying to engineer me into this relationship again. I was really scared. I thought, "I've got over all this – I can't go back to this again." So I kept well away from her.'

But Angela had not really 'adjusted to being heterosexual'. After she was married, she began to have full sexual relations with her husband. Her reaction to this was typical of many women: 'I enjoyed it – not physically but in the sense of relief that I'm doing whatever it is that I should be doing. He was quite easy to talk to about what worked me up, sexually. I was able to explain that putting something in and out just didn't have any effect on me at all. Then he was able to give me an orgasm manually. If he wanted sex, then I was going to have an orgasm. I wasn't thinking about being loved or loving him.'

Angela and her husband were Catholics. They did not use contraception and they had four children together, which Angela was, and still is, very happy about. But after the fourth child was born, she discovered that her husband had been 'having lots of girl-friends'. She had been monogamous herself, in body if not in spirit. She told her husband to leave and they applied for a divorce, with the approval of the priest. We wondered how she could contemplate divorce, especially as she had been a devout enough Catholic to obey the Church's ruling on contraception. 'I discussed it with the priest,' she explained 'and he said that it wasn't a marriage as my husband was never home and the best thing for everybody was a divorce.' It was only after her divorce that Angela, although she had always been convinced of her lesbianism, had her first fully sexual relationship with a woman. She met her first woman lover through an advertisement in *Time Out*. We asked her whether having sex with a woman was different from the sex she had had with her husband. 'Certainly was,' she answered with enthusiasm, 'yes, fantastic. Very relaxed. You could be yourself. You didn't have to perform – or be misunderstood. It's much easier to relate than to the male figure.' Outside bed, too, she went on, this new relationship was just what she had been looking for.

Finally we wanted to know from Angela what it's like to be a lesbian. 'I feel as if I'm in two worlds. At work I want to get them to understand me, and gradually get round to the subject and make them realize that gay people are nothing to be frightened of, rather than pitching in and saying, "You've jolly well got to accept gay people, we are all right." If they trust you they'll gradually get to know the information about you, and it's far more acceptable to them. I'm throwing out hints all the time and I'm watching reactions. I'm getting from one person : "I suppose you're gay and I don't really want to know." The difficulty is having children. If I was gay without children, I wouldn't feel I was living in two worlds. I would be gay and open about it. I've got to overcome greater obstacles, because of the children, in convincing people of the possibility of my being gay. People take it for granted, when you walk down the street with children, that you're heterosexual. This is what I mean about living in two worlds. Everywhere I go, where I'm not known, they're forcing me to behave as a heterosexual.'

We agreed with Angela that it is high time people stopped

assuming that a mother pushing a pram down the street is not a lesbian. She might just as well be lesbian as not, and the pressure of being 'forced to behave as a heterosexual' is very unpleasant for those who are not and do not want to be heterosexual.

We turn next to Penny who, like Angela, had been married and who told us quite plainly that she got married in order to 'get off the gay scene'. She had had three lesbian affairs before her marriage, one of which especially made a 'big impact'. It happened when Penny was fourteen. 'It was a sexual relationship, but she outgrew it and I didn't. We grew up together and I turned it into a sexual thing. She used to keep ranting on about this Brian. I took her into my room. I said, "Pretend I'm Brian." Anyway she fell for it. It happened a couple of times and then I think she began to feel as if she was a bit odd. And it came to a halt. And then she dropped me.'

Penny was puzzled about her feelings. She saw an opportunity to find out more during a biology lesson at school. 'They were explaining about the birds and the bees. They were speaking about sexual attraction, and I'd been dying to ask this question for such a long time. The teacher said, "Are there any questions?" So I said, "Yes, supposing one woman is attracted to another woman?" She said, "That's irrelevant. That doesn't enter into this discussion." This other girl said to me, "I've heard of them. They creep around. You can't mistake them." I said, "Why?" She said, "They've all got fat backsides." '

Needless to say, Penny went home after school and looked carefully in the mirror to see whether she had a fat backside! She hadn't. And she got no more information from anyone at school.

Soon afterwards, she left school and went to work in an office. There she overheard a conversation that prompted her to find out more : 'These two girls in the office were raving on about the fabulous time they'd had working in a holiday camp. The others said, "Those two girls, they were queers!" I thought, "Ah! Further investigation!" I wanted to find out, in any event, where I could meet somebody like myself. I got talking to the girls in the office. I said, "What about those funny girls?" Sort of working it into the conversation. They said, "Well, they're having it off, you know." Then I applied for a job in a holiday camp and got it. There I met Ann.' Penny was now fifteen. 'Along I trotted. On the way in, I spotted this blonde girl. And I thought, "Wow!" Anyway, I manipulated things and man-oeuvred and connived until I did move in with her. I thought she must be. I was sort of watching. And then I got friendly with her naturally. It was very nice, as you can imagine. You're getting paid to have a ball!

'We were there about five months. By this time, we were serious. This is where the crunch came, because we had been living together. Mum and Dad had popped down to see me – "We've got your room ready for you." "Oh," I said, "I thought of going on to work for Butlin's." Their faces were so disappoin-ted. They were all looking forward to my coming home. I took them a couple of presents home and I said, "I'm staying with Ann until she adapts herself to London." She took a long time adapting! My dad said, "You've got a lovely home. What's wrong with it?" I still didn't know what to say. There's nothing I could say. I think my mother had guessed. My dad asked, "Can I come and see where you're living?" This look, you know, it was terrible – he was so hurt. He came in. "And you prefer this to home?" And Mum said, "How can you prefer this to home?" I said, "Well, I don't . . ." I just floundered. And this would have carried on. But one night I went down to Bobby's, a gay club. You won't believe this! There was my mother! Ann nudged me and said, "Your mum's over there!" I said "So's Father Christmas!" But then my mum looked at me and I looked at her across the room. Can you imagine? She'd got her arm around this woman and I said, "Hello, how are you?" It was ridiculous! We were both stunned. Anyway, Ann and I sat down and spoke to her. She was with this woman she used to work with. I always thought she was rather fond of her. I didn't really know it was anything like that. I was worried about my dad's reaction – to both my mum's and my relationship. It was a most delicate situation. Obviously she discovered why I preferred to live with Ann. I didn't go round home for a week, being a coward. But I rang up. She said, "Oh, I understand things now, and I expect you do as well." I said, "Oh yes." '

This youthful relationship came to an end when Penny found

Ann sleeping with a man. Ann begged Penny not to leave her, but Penny felt too hurt to go on. It was after the end of this experience that she decided to marry and had her two children. The marriage broke down after the birth of her second child, she was divorced, and began a life of working to support her children. Some time after the divorce, she told us, she 'fell really in love with one woman – absolutely and completely.' She was still trying to get over it even though the relationship had ended seven years ago. 'I was really nuts over her,' she said. 'Her name was June. We were compatible in every way. Any arguments we had always ended up in a joke. After being together for five months, she moved in. Three months later she was killed outright in a car crash. Mara, a policewoman, called to inform me what had happened. She called on me regularly for the next year or so. But it was strictly platonic at that time. Eventually we became lovers and we lived together for four years, but I didn't feel the same towards Mara as I had felt towards June.'

Then Mara was promoted and transferred north. We asked whether the police had transferred them all as a family, and paid the moving costs. 'Oh no,' said Penny, 'it was all cloak and dagger. She would have lost her job. She was absolutely thrilled with this promotion. We'd discussed it greatly. "Should I go, Penny, shouldn't I go?" I was annoyed at her. She had to keep excusing me. We got a house in the country. I was angry inside. The police provided a house for her and her father. She treated me as a dark, deep secret after that. The kids and I weren't included in the lease. We moved at our own expense.'

In the Force, Mara had to pretend to be a single woman, and Penny had to act like a friend with two kids who just happened to be in the area. We asked about their social life. What had they done about police balls and social evenings? 'We used to go to them,' said Penny. 'I just sat in the corner.'

The pressure of living in such secrecy was too much of a burden on the relationship and in the end Penny and her children moved back to London. Although she is nearly forty, Penny is still searching for a lasting relationship. 'Ideally,' she admitted, 'I would like to meet somebody to share my life with me.'

Angela and Penny each discovered their lesbian potential early in adolescence and in a private way. Their romantic and sexual feelings were aroused spontaneously by members of their own sex. The same things did not happen to Rachel. Her lesbian feelings were aroused when she was already adult. At the time she was living, and still lives, in a squat. It is a semi-detached house in a city, which Rachel shares with two other women and her son Peter, who is still a toddler. The household is run on loose communal lines, the occupants sharing most of their resources. Sometimes one or other of the women has a lover living with her.

We met Amy at the same time as we talked to Rachel and she described their situation for us: 'There are four of us who live in the house. Cassandra, upstairs, has her own kitchen and is more or less independent. Then the three of us, Rachel, my girl-friend Ellen, who's in Canada now, and myself, live in the down-stairs of the house with Peter. We came to be living here more or less accidentally because we were all looking for a place at the same time. We're in Wages Due Lesbians together. So we just happened to find this place and as a result of that we do share some things. We don't share it in an organized kind of way. We don't have rotas or things like that. We are all lesbians.'

Rachel added that she and Amy were the two most responsible for bringing up Peter, but that they did not have a lesbian rela-tionship together. They work together in Wages Due Lesbians, an independent group of lesbian women who organize within Wages for Housework, particularly in regard to custody. Wages for Housework is an international organization fighting for money for all women so that they can lead independent lives. Rachel and Amy share the bills, the food and the kitchen work. Each of them – including Peter – has her own room.

'We don't pay rent because it's a squat,' Amy told us. 'We share bills three ways. Cassandra has her own bills, except for the telephone. Whoever has more money, buys more things, but we don't have a set amount to put in for housekeeping and things like that. We're very lackadaisical about it, but it seems to sort itself out. Some days, somebody will do the shopping, and some-body does the cooking.'

We were interested to know how these women had come to be lesbians. We asked Rachel first, and she told us that she had had her first lesbian relationship when she was seven months

pregnant. 'I had sort of resigned myself to having a sexless pregnancy. The bloke was away. I fell in love with this woman. It
was really nice. And she was there at the birth.' We asked if she
had felt any attraction towards women before this, and she
answered, 'I'd felt it, but I hadn't really thought about it. When
I was doing midwifery, I was pretty fed up. I wanted to be with
women. I wanted to organize with women. I thought the way
to do it was through getting a paid job, going on a hospital ward,
but I just ended up doing piles of unpaid work in gruelling conditions. I was exhausted all the time. If somebody's off sick, you
get an extra load of work and you're always fighting each other.
Then I came in contact with the Wages for Housework campaign. Wages Due Lesbians was a very public part of it and
it opened up a whole new range of possibilities for me that I'd
never thought about before. I wanted to do something about my
shitty life, living in a squat, having no money, and doing unpaid
housework on the ward and at home. Doing eight hours' shift
work and being exhausted didn't seem like getting anywhere.

'The woman I first lived with – she'd decided she was lesbian
from since she'd been about three and she'd never had relationships with men and she thought that lesbians never could be
mothers and that lesbians were childless. She'd never had any
maternal feelings herself, she'd never considered the possibility –
it just seemed out of the question. She really liked Peter, he sort
of became her child – she really liked it. A lot of lesbian women
block out the idea of ever having a child.'

When the father of Rachel's baby came back and found
Rachel in a lesbian relationship, he decided he still wanted her.
But she told him to leave, so he went abroad. After two months
he returned again, but again she asked him to leave. 'When he
came back, there we were, the three of us stuck together,
poverty-stricken, about to tear each other to pieces; it was freezing cold – it was a cold winter. She was foreign, he was an immi-
grant. For the first few days the three of us would go around
together – very jolly – we got on all right. I kept thinking, "I
wonder how long this is going to last?" – and they had their
arms around each other. At night they would alternate. She
would sleep downstairs one night, and then he did. That lasted
one week. Then there was this incredible blow-up. I didn't fuck

with him. I didn't want to. I did an enormous amount of emotional housework with him, listening to him for hours. He thought that eventually my lover would sleep with him.'

We asked if he had suggested that all three of them should sleep together, because that is a common fantasy among men; they often imagine that what two lesbians really want is to share their relationship with a man. Rachel's male lover had indeed made this suggestion. 'That really took his fancy,' she said. 'He couldn't stand it that she wasn't a bit interested in him. We had terrible scenes. This went on for three weeks. She [her lover] got attacks of asthma. It was pretty traumatic. We somehow managed to organize ourselves. She went and stayed somewhere else. She'd be sitting up all night unable to breathe. Then I'd drive back home and he was ranting and raving.

'Eventually he went off to Spain. She and I tried to get our relationship back, but it had been too traumatic. She was exhausted by the whole thing. She couldn't take any more, so she went back to Mexico. Then he came back. I kept thinking there must be some way we could be friends. I'd known him for about six or seven years. I wanted him to accept I was lesbian. I thought he would be able to. I wanted to be able to share the child, but not sleep with him. But he kept refusing that. There was this tug-of-war situation. I wanted him to look after the child, but I was scared of him getting too close to the child, because he would become too attached to us. I was playing two things all the time. Then I moved into this squat; that really said to him, quite clearly, that I didn't want to set up house with him. He realized then that I didn't want to live with men any more.'

After this the father had not come back, but Rachel took Peter to Spain to visit him. She explained that she wants the boy to know his father, but that the father would not be able to cope if Rachel met him with her woman lover. Rachel thinks that Peter's father can deal better with her lesbianism if he is in his own country. She has no animosity towards this man, describing him as 'a very likeable extravert character, very spontaneous, warm and generous'.

Rachel's friend and colleague, Amy, discovered her lesbian potential primarily through the consciousness-raising she experienced from her engagement with the feminist movement. 'Coming out' was a very important step for her.

'It meant I said I was a lesbian. I'd been thinking about it for a year or two; I had slept with a woman. I also felt some pressure from the feminist movement that to be a lesbian, you had to be a certain way – like have short hair and ride motor bikes. If you had long hair and wore dresses, you somehow weren't lesbian. Even though I had been attracted to women, I felt I couldn't be like that. Until I'd slept with a woman, I'd felt somehow I wasn't lesbian.'

What Amy needed to resolve for herself was, first, that the public stereotype of the mannish woman did not actually describe the range of lesbian possibilities, and, secondly, that sexual experience with a woman was somehow a necessary step in her identification of herself as a lesbian. This experience changed her consciousness, but not her sense of identity.

'Afterwards,' she explained, 'there was no difference, it was just that I could say I was. It wasn't as if I'd changed my personality or the way I thought. Up till then I'd been sleeping with men – and liked sleeping with men – but in the women's movement, even if you were attracted to women and you were sleeping with men, there was something a bit kookie about you! Obviously I felt conflict.'

Clearly, Amy did not feel she was unable to form relationships with men, but her feminist convictions were so important to her that she transferred her sexual feelings to women without any evidence of psychological trauma. Furthermore, her experiences of helping to bring up Peter have encouraged her own maternal feelings and she told us that she is now considering having her own child. 'I've thought about AID,' she told us, 'but I'm not sure what I'd tell the child about who the father was. I'm thinking about hetero-sex. I'm not convinced either way yet. It's being around Peter makes a lot of difference. I haven't done anything about it yet, except buy babies' clothes!'

Both Rachel and Amy insisted that their way of living had greater meaning for them than the expression of their individuality. It also had political meaning. Rachel explained: 'I mean you are supposed to live with men in society. And supposed to look after men and do all that work. We're not doing that. And

boys are supposed to have a father that they can identify with.
We are stepping out of line. I think we're doing what all women
are doing, we're refusing to be the sort of woman the state wants
– the sort of mother the state wants – the perfect housewife.
Wherever women are stepping out of line, it is a threat to the
establishment.'

Rachel and Amy had one further, and ironic, comment to
add. Just as heterosexual society assumes that all mothers are
heterosexual women, so, it seems, do many lesbians. Rachel said
she had had to do 'a lot of work' to prove to her lesbian friends
that she really was a lesbian. And Amy pointed out that out of
the lesbians she had met, she could count on one hand the
number who had never slept with men.

For Rachel and Amy, then, exploring their lesbian potential
was correlated much more with their feminist principles than
with any psychosexual rejection of men. Furthermore, Amy's
desire to have a child had been stimulated by her lesbian context, rather than negated by it.

The story of Lila, a single mother of three, provides a significant contrast to that of Rachel and Amy. Lila is a Jamaican who
came to Britain at the age of twenty-one. Unlike Rachel and
Amy, who were able to make conscious decisions about their
sexuality, Lila responded, finally, to feelings she first became
aware of in early adolescence. 'I remember fancying the teacher
at school first,' she told us. 'She had a sister. Every time she
passed I'd go up to the top of the hill and watch her and admire
her. My other friends talked about boys, but it was no interest
to me. I turned to men because I couldn't get a woman. In
Jamaica we don't talk about it. I never met another lesbian.
If you see a girl you fancy, you keep quiet about it. You don't
want other girls to know. The only time I heard it talked about
was in school by boys about boys, because there were some
Englishmen, who had a slaughterhouse, and these boys said
they could get money off them. So I put two and two together.
Then when I came over here, I don't hear anybody talk about
it either.'

We asked Lila if she had had any lesbian relationships since
she had been in Britain. 'Yes,' she answered, 'only one. April
gone one year – eighteen months ago. It was the first time. I

had a boy-friend who was coming and going. I remember one night lying there and I couldn't stand him to touch me or anything. A piece of paper dropped through my door with something about homosexual. I don't know for what reason but I put it aside. In the morning I just got up out of that bed and ran downstairs and searched for that bit of paper. I found it and rang up the number. I thought, "God, I can't go on any more, gotta find a woman. I can't go on living with a man." I think I was going to scream, just lying there with him. Anyway, I rang the number. It was a local CHE [Campaign for Homosexual Equality] group. I went there. I wasn't very happy, I was the only woman there. Then I met two white girls there later and they tell me about this coloured girl who sometimes comes to meetings. She was bisexual, because she was married. It was my first affair. It wasn't hers. I wasn't disappointed. I didn't fall in love with her. I like her. We are still good friends. She has this girl-friend she met before me. This girl-friend is mine as well. We are good friends too.'

We asked Lila if she had enjoyed sex with the fathers of her three children. 'It was awful,' she replied, 'just as a part of going with a man. I think I only went with them because I was frustrated. It wasn't painful. The body horrifies me and the penis. Funny, I've never curled up beside a man, or kissed them or hugged them. With women, it's a feeling of excitement when I touch them. Especially if she's tall and slim, my knees turn to jelly. I don't know what it is about them – I'm in hysterics.' We pressed Lila on this point. If she had not enjoyed sex with men, why had she gone on having male lovers? 'Because I couldn't get a woman,' she replied simply. Then we asked if masturbation had helped her feeling of frustration. 'One time I do it, but it does nothing for me,' she said. She added that the first time she had slept with a woman it had felt natural and beautiful.

Lila was prompted by a CHE pamphlet to face her lesbian needs. Sandra was prompted by a television documentary. Sandra lives with her second husband, Ben, and Jack, the ten-year-old son of her first marriage. Sandra and Ben watched the documentary together and for some weeks afterwards Sandra had the subject on her mind. 'I've always been truthful,' she told us. 'Ben and me've always been truthful to one another. I

Rocking the Cradle

was always thinking, "Shall I tell him, shall I not?" I thought, "I've had one broken marriage – I've gone through one – I might as well go through another one." Then I decided to tell him. I thought, "One of two things can happen. Either Ben is going to shout his head off or he's going to thump me." It was gone twelve o'clock at night and I done it in the kitchen. I purposely told him after twelve o'clock because 1) he can't shout at me because of the neighbours, and 2) he can't hit me, again because of the neighbours. I sat down and said to him, "Have you noticed anything different over the last few weeks?" He said to me, "How do you mean? Well, you've been very snappy, short-tempered." So I said, "Have you noticed anything else?" He looked at me and I said, "Now take a good look at me." He laughed. It was a nervous laugh. He said, "I've noticed you've been pinching my shirts." (I was wearing one of them – he's the same size as me, you see.) I said, "What conclusion have you come to?" then, "Before you say any more, what I've got to tell you, you'll probably want a divorce." He sat there. Then he said, "I've come to my own conclusion." "Yes, say it. I'm not going to say it. It's got to come from your mouth." He said, " I think you're a lesbian." I said, " Yes, what are your views on it? Are you going to thump me?" "No, what am I going to thump you for? You haven't done anything wrong." "Do you want a divorce?" "No, not really." "You're quite prepared then?" "Yes." So that's how it came out.'

When we asked Sandra whether she had had any lesbian relationships she told us that when she was fifteen she had had an affair with a girl at her school. After she was divorced from her first husband, she had had another lesbian affair. We asked whether she had liked boys when she was young. She explained that she had not been sexually interested in boys, but that she had always played 'with a gang of boys, right from seven onwards'. She was a tomboy. 'I was with boys, it was always boys,' she said. 'Cowboys and Indians. I had to have a cowboy outfit, not a cowgirl outfit. I liked playing their games.' Sandra went on to explain that there was a difference in her feelings between the love she had had for her first girl-friend and the way she had felt about her first husband. 'I think I was deeper in love with the girl than what I was with my husband,' she told us. 'I got on all right with him. It wasn't the same sort of love as it was for the girl.' What had the sexual relationship been like with her husband? 'Sometimes I would feel very sick,' she replied. 'I just didn't fancy a man pawing me.' Had she felt sexual pleasure? 'No.' She had taken part 'because he wanted to. In the beginning it was painful. That stopped after a time. I relaxed more and I got used to it.'

We asked Ben when it had first occurred to him that Sandra might be a lesbian and he said, 'When that TV programme was on.' He had had 'slight doubts' before that, but it was the programme which made him think he must 'bring her out to admit it'. He went on, 'I knew it wasn't easy for her to admit this, but I had to try and get her to come out so I niggled her. I was really interested in the subject.' We wondered how he had felt when she had 'admitted' it. 'It doesn't worry me,' he said. 'After seeing the TV show, and having a talk with her, I understand much more about it now. It doesn't hurt me. I accept it. It's something she can't help. It's something inside her. The way you're born, I suppose.' We asked Ben if he would be upset by Sandra having a relationship with a woman. He said he would not. But if she had a relationship with another man, he would be upset – 'funnily enough', he added.

Lilian and Mary have been living together for eighteen years. Each of them had been married and Lilian had two sons when they formed a friendship. Lilian had not had any experience of homosexuality. 'When I left school, I went to the Poly,' she told us. 'I never knew anything about homosexuality. I had never heard about people being gay. When I was at the Poly – about sixteen or seventeen – one of the fellows told me, rambling in Regent's Park between exams, about homosexuals. I said, "No! Really? Show me one." I didn't know anything about it. I had girl-friends, certainly, but no more than that.'

We asked Lilian if she had been surprised to fall in love with Mary. 'Yes,' she responded, 'I was astonished.' Mary added, 'We got on very well together, didn't we? It was a super sort of friendship – and then there was a sort of tension. I couldn't quite figure this out. I couldn't work it out at all. I remember one night – I hadn't been staying with Lilian's family very long in Canada – I remember I was going out with somebody – a

Spanish gent – and you' (pointing to Lilian) 'slapped me round the face – do you remember?' 'Mmm,' Lilian mumbled. 'I was surprised,' Mary went on. 'And yet I wasn't. I didn't react normally as you would when a straight girl-friend hits you. She didn't say why. Yet I knew it was because I was going out with this fellow. Nothing had been said, done, touched or anything. I didn't ring him up to say where I was going to meet him. I didn't go out.'

Lilian took up the story: 'Before that, a couple of months, everybody was working. Mary was working, Eric [Lilian's husband] was working and I was looking after the kids and cooking. I was washing up – and it hit me like a bomb – I was in love with her. That was the first thing. Then I thought, "Where do we go from here?" I had to figure it out – on no knowledge or nothing – what it's all about. It appeared to make me lesbian, but I thought, "What do they do?" Well, I'd figured that out by the time I'd finished the washing-up. It took a week from that moment on. As a person, I don't hang around. I'd rather push in and see what happens, rather than make sure everything's lovely first. I'd pretty well figured out I wasn't going to get the cold shoulder, anyway. We went to one of those awful Canadian shower parties. We had one or two in the pub first, and this place was high on the mountain. I was loaded and took the car down at eighty. When we got to the bottom, I just fell on her and away we went.' Mary broke in: 'I had met lesbians before. I hadn't done anything about it. Obviously, I hadn't met anybody I fancied. I was married then – it had never occurred to me.'

We asked Mary if she thought she had *become* a lesbian, so to speak. She explained, 'I think I was a potential lesbian – yes, from the word go, really. I always had friendships my mother wanted to break up, and my friends were always jealous of my other friends. I had stirrings and fancied people, but I never did anything about it.' Had she been satisfied in her heterosexual life? 'Not really,' she said. 'It was all right.' Had she loved her husband? 'Yes, at the time I did,' she answered. What had been different when she met Lilian? 'Well,' she replied, 'it felt the right sort of thing for me. I can remember pushing all these things to the back of my mind and I didn't have to any more.' We then asked both women if either of them had wanted, since they had been together, to go back to men? 'No,' said Mary. 'It was absolutely right to be a lesbian, and I'm sorry it didn't happen sooner. I would have had a happier life.' And Lilian added, 'Marvellous. Absolutely – never go back to men.'

Of all the women we met, Kath and Vera were the ones who had made a relationship with each other at the earliest age. They were in the same class at school and formed a friendship which got 'closer and closer', Kath said. She added, however, that 'there was no hint of any sexual relations. It never occurred to us we were other than good friends. In between leaving school and university I had relationships with men.' Vera continued, 'In retrospect I think I felt bad about the relationships Kath was having with men. We lived together for six months quite happy as very close friends. We even shared the same bed.' We pressed Kath to say whether she had really been interested in men. She said that she had; for about two years she had enjoyed men sexually and had taken contraceptives. 'What brought about a change in this rather ambiguous situation was the death of my father. I realized during that awful time that Vera was the only person who could really offer me anything valuable. I suppose that made us realize the full extent of our relationship and the depth of it. My mother accepted and still accepts Vera as a close school friend.'

Although Kath and Vera are still in their mid-twenties, they have already lived together for five years, have their toddler Katy and are expecting Kath's second child. During the early part of this period together, Kath explained, they had to explore what to do. 'I had left college early,' she said. 'We did not want jobs because we wanted to be together all the time and yet we could not be together because we needed money. So for the next year we joined various community groups. This gave us an opportunity to be together and do the things together that we found interesting and rewarding. Then we went to Bristol for a few months. We joined a women's liberation group and were involved with the abortion campaign and other action groups.'

We asked if they had adjusted to being lesbian. 'There was no adjustment,' said Kath. Vera agreed: 'It grew over such a long period of time.' Then Kath expanded, 'We meet many gay women and I can see many of their problems linked to that one traumatic realization – that they are homosexual in a society which condemns such an orientation. It was very different for us, in that our relationship grew very gradually into a sexual one. There was no realization of being gay. It was inextricably related to the friendship, concern and love we felt for one another. A gay consciousness as such developed later and in relation to feminism. Had we been less open to alternative orientation generally, or in this case sexually, I suppose we might never have gone beyond the friendship level. As it was, the progress seemed perfectly natural. Obviously there is a distinction between our feelings about our relationship and others' attitudes towards it. We have encountered negative attitudes, naturally, and in some ways they hit us harder because of our own lack of guilt feelings. Related to this, a vital thing that most people find very difficult to do, is to get away from their families. It affects the rest of their lives and you see middle-aged people, not just gays, who are unable to make that break. I suppose I had some advantages in making that break in that as a child I was given an unusual degree of independence. This was related to the particular patterns of relationships in my family and, while it was a positive force enabling me to achieve independence of thought and action, it also had its negative aspects because of its largely coincidental nature and it led to some insecurity. I was able, though, at a relatively early age, to look at my parents outside their parental role. That was a crucial point, really, and while I could never be objective, I was able to step very slightly back from the family situation and see them as people to be approached on that level.'

So far it seems clear that there are only two things that all these women have in common – first, they are, or want to become, mothers, and, second, they enjoy sexual relationships with other women. But the stimulus to their lesbian experiences has been different and various. For some women, strong emotional attachments to other girls, early in their adolescence, enabled them to develop their lesbian sexuality, although a sexual adjustment to men remained a social prerogative. For others, falling in love with a woman was an experience which came only with adulthood and after having entered heterosexual commitments. For still others, the growth of a feminist conscious-

ness significantly broadened their awareness of a lesbian alternative, which was eagerly sought. Yet in spite of these very different
paths leading to the same result of lesbian pairing, all the women
described their lesbian experiences as good and natural. We
were interested in finding out, therefore, whether that sense of
naturalness had spilled over into their relationships with their
children, or whether, as might be expected, social disapproval
of lesbianism had led to these women feeling a conflict between
their sense of adequacy as mothers and their sense of fulfilment
as lesbians. The ages of the women ranged from the early twenties
to the middle fifties; the ages of their children ranged from
infancy to the early twenties. Since some women had been
mothers for much longer than others, some of the replies given
by the younger mothers were more theoretical – orientated towards planning for the upbringing of their children – whereas
the older mothers spoke more of the effects and responses already
obvious in their children.

Lilian's sons, for example, are both now in their twenties.
When Lilian and Mary met in Canada and made a relationship
together, Lilian's sons were six and four years old. Lilian and
Mary left Lilian's husband and children and went to live in a
flat in the same town. Lilian's husband stayed in the house with
the boys and a housekeeper. He sued his wife for custody and
won. Eventually he sold the house in Canada, came back to
England, and arranged for the two boys to live with his sister.
Mary and Lilian stayed on in Canada. We asked Lilian if this
had caused her much conflict. 'Very much so,' she said. 'I was
very unhappy about this.' Mary added, 'It was very difficult.
Although Lilian hasn't said it, it wasn't a particularly happy
marriage. She couldn't have taken the children anyway, because
she'd been a housewife. She hadn't a job. It was very difficult at
that time to get a job in Canada. She got a job before she left
[the house] and I had a job, but we couldn't possibly have
afforded to take on the children at their age. We lived in a little
flat with two armchairs, we didn't have any facilities for children. Eric [Lilian's husband] could afford the housekeeper and
the house, so there was no question about where the children
were better off. We discussed this a lot. I was in a very peculiar
position. I didn't like it very much. Lilian said she didn't care,

she had to live with me. There it was. At the same time, Lilian
wanted the children to go back to England, because the relatives
were there and because the education was better.'

They decided, eventually, to return to England themselves, and
arrived at Waterloo Station with nine pounds between them.
'Mary went to her mum,' Lilian continued. 'I went to my mum,
who wasn't very pleased. All my friends and family rushed
around in smaller and smaller circles writing to each other and
having long conferences, hysterics and everything, as to why I
had mucked up this marvellous marriage. I didn't say anything.'
Then followed a custody battle in the English courts during
which time, a whole year, the boys lived with Eric's sister. Their
father visited them at weekends and Lilian went down to see
them and occasionally to take them back to the flat she shared
with Mary. Jack, the younger boy, was very miserable and once
said to Mary, 'Do you think if I came to London and got a job,
I could stay with you and Mummy?' 'It was heart-breaking,'
Lilian said. 'I was going berserk trying to move the courts to
get custody.' Eventually Eric decided he couldn't manage the
responsibility of his sons and he asked Lilian if she would take
over. She agreed readily and the court made the necessary order.
From then on the boys lived with Lilian and Mary.

Gradually Lilian and Mary began to meet other lesbians but
because of the children, Lilian explained, they felt they should
pretend to be heterosexual. For the purposes of social meetings
with relatives and married friends, they thought up stories about
boy-friends who were married. They did not admit to the children that they had a lesbian relationship. We asked if they slept
apart when the boys were with them. Lilian replied that they
had had a large bedroom with a double bed and a single bed.

Then, when Jack was nine, they discovered that he was
dyslexic; he still couldn't read, even though he had a high IQ.
We asked Lilian if she thought her lesbianism and her leaving
the family had contributed to this problem. She replied, 'I had
suffered constantly, since the moment I packed off and left my
old man. But I've never had one . . . *one* . . . qualm of guilt
about that, never. I've never had that about being lesbian. It's
been absolutely marvellous. It's so right that I felt, "Why the hell
was I so thick not to realize it before?" I had always felt, until

very recently, very guilty about walking out on my kids. I've lived with that for years. I feel that children are so defenceless. I mean you wouldn't take an animal in and then just drop it. If you give birth to a child or adopt it — I can't differentiate between birth, adoption, or taking in someone else's child — if it happens to be your responsibility, you actually know that and it stays with you until it dissipates itself with the children's age, or whatever. It's inside you, where people belong to you, and it affects you.'

Since she had these views, had Lilian felt that she had a choice when she left Eric for Mary? 'Personally, no,' she replied. 'I can't live any sort of lie. Not with my sort of nature. I suppose Mary and I have, for some years, by being gay and pretending to be straight, but that was for other people, that wasn't for ourselves. I mean, let me give you an example. After I'd married Eric — sexually he was a bit of a tired hat : one hump a month — I had an affair with a smashing bloke, quietly, on the side. Gosh, he made me laugh a lot and I got somewhat pregnant. I could not possibly have had another child and remained with my husband and said it was his. So I aborted one night.'

When had Lilian and Mary told the boys that they were lovers? Lilian said that she thought they had known for some time. 'I sat down and told Jack. He'd just come back from Kenya. "You've probably known this all along but I'm gay." He fell about laughing. He was about eighteen then. I told Valk later. I didn't make a long tiddly of it, you know, and I never went into great discussions about it. I was tidying up a bit. They were adult. I don't like to live a lie with people I love. Now Jack is twenty-one, Valk is twenty-three. They are both straight.'

We asked Lilian if she thought her being a lesbian had had a bad effect on her sons. 'I really couldn't say,' she answered. 'It's terribly difficult. I have thought about that. I don't know.' Mary added, 'I don't think so. They really love Lilian.' Lilian then went on, 'We did all the normal and ordinary things that are expected to be done for children by parents. Like turning up at school — the pantomimes and theatres, whatever.' Mary continued, 'And we wore hats and gloves — I was known as "Auntie Mary"!' Lilian broke in, 'We went on the way everyone else

did. And Mary's famous cooking. They used to come home for
weekends in long trousers and bring their friends – and by God,
did those kids eat – and scented baths they always used to
have . . .' 'Yes,' said Mary, 'my scent. . . .'

Did they have an opinion about whether or not lesbians ought
to be mothers? 'I think it's up to the individual, really,' replied
Lilian. 'There are so many bad mothers, so many kids in care,
who the hell's to stand up and say that a lesbian can't be a
better mother than somebody else? It's madness.' 'I see no reason
why lesbians shouldn't have children,' Mary added. 'Lilian was a
good mother to her kids. She didn't always bring them up as I
would wish; they often ate their peas on the wrong side of the
fork! But the boys quite obviously love Lilian. And if they're
in any trouble, they come here, talk to her and whatever. I
think they're fond of me. So what's wrong with lesbian mothers?'

Angela has four children, of whom the eldest is a daughter of
sixteen. When we asked if she had told her children about her
lesbianism, she answered, 'I'll tell my eldest daughter if she
asks me, but she doesn't want to know intimate details. I am
nervous of discussing this aspect openly with the children. I feel
I don't have to tell the children – they know. They pick it up –
they see it. With May [a former lover] we used to watch television with all the children and I'd lie on the settee with my head
in May's lap. In that sense, I'm open. I don't hide anything.
Rather than saying to the children, "Now look here, I'm what
is called a lesbian." It doesn't matter what your sex life is, the
most important thing is to love your children. To have an open
mind about all sorts of things. As long as you don't keep yourself
and them closeted away from mixing with friends and their
families, so that the children have a chance to see the spectrum
of the whole world as it is.' We asked Angela if she would be
bothered by any of her children growing up to be homosexual,
to which she replied that it wouldn't bother her at all.

Anne and Liz have two small children. We asked them
whether they thought there were any reasons why lesbians ought
not to have children. 'Research is the only way to find out,'
answered Liz. Would they be willing, then, for their children to
be part of a research programme? Liz said she wouldn't object
as long as she knew what it was for and what it entailed. Anne,

the mother of the children, did not agree. 'I don't want it,' she said. 'They grow up like anybody else.' We put it to her that 'growing up like anybody else' suggested that they would be heterosexual. 'Well, yes, that's sexually speaking,' Liz said. 'When Anne says they grow up like anyone else, I think they grow up a lot better, and less sexist. On the homosexuality side, *we* certainly wouldn't mind it – it's a valid alternative.' We then asked how they would answer someone saying that if they had a homosexual child, it would be because they were lesbians. 'I wouldn't bother about what anybody says,' replied Liz. 'If we bothered about what anybody said, we wouldn't be this far now.'

We suggested next that many people seemed particularly anxious about what would happen to the sons of lesbians, since they assumed that boys in particular needed a male model to follow. What was going to happen to their son, growing up without such a father figure in the house? 'He's going to be much nicer!' Anne replied promptly. 'He's got his gender sorted out,' Liz added. 'We didn't fuss about gender when he was younger because we didn't want him to be sexist. We asked a psychologist friend who thought we were wrong not to give him good ideas about gender. But in fact James has got gender very strongly, whether we pressed it or not. He's got the television, he plays with other kids in other households.'

Anne and Liz live in a fairly remote part of the country. In these circumstances, how open or closed had they decided their relationship should appear? 'We don't go out of our way to show affection, or not to show it,' said Liz. 'We sleep in the same bed. We call it mama's bed.' Did they let the children come into their bed in the morning? 'We are all four in the bed at least half the night!' replied Liz. Outside the home, they explained, there were not 'big social goings on'. Close friends knew about their relationship and one of them said to Liz and Anne, 'You're just a boring middle-aged married couple!'

Then we enquired if the children had asked any questions yet. James had asked who his father was, Liz told us. 'The story we told him,' Anne explained, 'was that Father was just a friend and we were fond of each other, that we didn't want to live together and he went away to be an engineer.' Liz said she told him, ' "Everybody's got a daddy; some daddies live with them and some don't." Actually, we try to use the word "father", rather than "daddy", because "daddy" is such a relationship word, whereas "father" is a bit more remote.' How did James react? 'Oh, he thought about it,' said Anne. 'He tends to take things in and then he'll talk about it,' Liz continued. 'I was reading him a story one night afterwards and it ended up with the mother putting a child to bed. He asked, "Where's his daddy then?" I said, "Perhaps his father doesn't live with him." Because daddy wasn't mentioned in the book.' Anne commented, 'Daddies are so idealized in children's stories.'

Our next question was whether Anne would tell her daughter, who was conceived through AID, the same story as she told James. 'We had a think about that,' she replied. 'I think she's going to get the same story, for the time being, until they're old enough to understand.' Did that mean that they intended to tell the truth one day? 'I disagree with putting more on children than they're able to cope with,' Liz said. 'I'm against overloading them with lots of information. We want to answer their questions.' Anne added, 'And they'll assume they have the same father.'

Did it bother *them* that the children had different fathers? 'I'd prefer them to be brother and sister,' Liz admitted, but Anne pointed out, 'My sister is my half-sister. I've never thought of her as other than my sister.' Liz then commented that Anne and her half-sister were much closer to each other than Liz was to her own two sisters.

Next, we wondered how Anne and Liz would react if the children were to bring friends home and say, 'These are my two mums and they're lesbians?' Liz disagreed immediately with our wording. 'He doesn't see me as his second mother,' she said. What did the boy call her then? 'Liz,' she replied. 'He calls Anne "Anne" at the moment, and "Mama". We don't see ourselves advertising an alternative lifestyle. Probably what we will do is the same as we've done, particularly with our families. We've never discussed it but it is accepted.'

Later we shall consider what some of the children themselves have to say about their mothers' ways of living. From the women, however, we did not receive any impressions of special guilt or

anxiety about the development of their children. They seemed
to have a protective concern for the welfare of their children
which could be expected of any responsible parents. Nor did they
offer any theoretical views which could be described as specifically
lesbian; that is, views of parenthood which could not equally
be found amongst a group of heterosexual mothers. Kath
expressed this in some detail : 'I see being lesbian as about being
a woman, caring for women, loving them. It therefore accords
a higher place to motherhood and child-rearing. Understand-
ably, perhaps, feminism in its initial stages involved a rejection
of these traditionally feminine roles which were seen as oppressive.
I feel we now need to begin a reappraisal of this and strive for
an awareness of the liberating and positive aspects of these roles.
As far as I am concerned, feminism is not about emulating
traditional male values; it is about a re-evaluation of the female
model. Feminine virtues such as the nurturant role, intuitive
powers of women and so on have been secondary for too long.
While having children is a much more deeply rooted and less
rational need for me than this theorizing might suggest, it certainly does not conflict with any philosophy or any consciousness of being gay or feminist. I have worries which are not
directly linked to any sexual orientation but are concerned with
our whole philosophy about bringing up a child. This is not to
say that I do not worry about other people's attitudes towards
two gay women bringing up a child, but this is only one of the
considerations, for I feel many people would be critical of our
whole philosophy. We believe that every child should be brought
up so that from as early as possible they take responsibility for
their own actions and decisions. That is not to say that they are
given indiscriminate freedom but that within a secure frame-
work they are encouraged to think for themselves and to decide
for themselves whenever possible. Not surprisingly this puts us
at odds with conventional education where the emphasis is on
imposed rather than self-discipline and engenders a whole array
of other prejudices, rigid attitudes and so on.'

The idea that lesbian sexuality and motherhood might be
conflicting drives or might be incompatible emotional areas in
a woman's life is not one which received any reinforcement from
the lesbian women we met. Indeed, they accepted these two

experiences as being entirely natural to them, and to such an unconscious degree that we were unable, in spite of asking very direct questions, to uncover any material that would help to disarm the prejudices of those who think that lesbianism necessarily precludes, or should preclude, motherhood. Time and again we asked the women what they would say to people who think lesbians are not able to be adequate mothers. Equally often we received the same answer that Liz gave : 'I wouldn't bother about what anybody says. If we bothered about what anybody said, we wouldn't be this far now.' Equally often, too, lesbian mothers echoed the judgement of one woman who wrote to us : 'People's criticisms are caused by *their* inadequacies, not mine. I just pity their lack of tolerance.'

Even though these women became mothers under widely different circumstances, and even though some had consciously wanted to have children and others had just fallen into it, they accepted their motherhood as an entirely natural development for them – for their personalities and for their womanhood. Nor did their becoming mothers dissuade them from their lesbianism – if anything, motherhood reinforced their desire to make relationships with women. In some cases, too, lesbian lovers living with lesbian mothers found their own maternal longings reinforced and at the time of the conversations we record here, several of these women were planning to have children of their own. It seemed, therefore, that the lack of conflict which the mothers described was demonstrated in their experiences; for themselves and for their lovers, lesbian needs and maternal needs reinforced and affirmed one another.

3 Courts of Flaw

Lesbian mothers are often women who become mothers within a conventional marriage and, when such marriages end in divorce, have to face the problem of what will happen to their children when wife and husband separate. An increasing number of heterosexual parents are also enduring this particular agony, but what is different for lesbians is that the judicial system nearly always awards custody to the father when a custody case is contested by a lesbian mother. The attitude of the courts is exemplified by a House of Lords judgement in 1976 : 'Changes in public attitudes should not entitle the courts to relax in any degree the vigilance and severity with which they should regard the risk of children at critical ages being exposed or introduced to ways of life which may lead to severance from normal society, to psychological stresses and unhappiness and possibly even to physical experience which may scar them for life.'

Heterosexual mothers, as is well known, are nearly always awarded custody. The idea that lesbianism *per se* is accepted as grounds for deciding that a woman is an unfit mother has caused extreme distress for many lesbians and their children and is a principal reason for the fear lesbian mothers have that their children might be taken away from them if their lesbian sexuality becomes common knowledge. Consequently, they try to keep their sexuality secret, or, when angry husbands find out about it, allow themselves to be blackmailed and threatened and even abused, so long as they feel they have some chance of keeping their children.

The extent of this fear and humiliation is extreme and the treatment some of these women have endured at the hands of their erstwhile loving husbands, sanctioned by the judicial authorities, can only be described as shocking. The fear is so widespread that it extends even beyond marriage. Rachel, who has never been married, told us, for example, that she had not put the name of the father of her son on the child's birth certificate, even though the father acknowledged paternity. 'I had a lot of wise advice from Wages Due Lesbians not to put his name on the birth certificate. I'm really glad I didn't, because if I had, he could take Peter to Spain and I could never get him back.' We asked her whether she would advise other lesbian mothers to do the same. 'Oh yes,' she said, 'any mother. It's just that if you're a mother on your own and you don't want to have custody hassles, to minimize them, it's just sensible not to name the father. I do think kids, generally, do belong to their mother, anyway. We're the ones who are entitled to them, because we look after them and care for them. Which is not to say that fathers should be shoved out of the back door. I mean it is women who make the decision to carry the child and have it.'

We asked how the Department of Health and Social Security had reacted to this decision. 'I was very silly, actually,' Rachel said. 'I gave them his name. It was a man [from the DHSS]. He treated me like a slut because I wasn't married. I wanted to defend myself by saying I knew who the father was. Then I had a visit from the doctor who's the head of the surgery. You never see him, only the doctors below him. I asked him why he'd come. "Oh, routine visit. Where's Peter? I'd like to see him." He said he'd heard Peter was run down and wanted me to bring him to the surgery tomorrow. So I went and took a friend. I was very glad I did. He asked me lots of questions: Was I a single mother? What sort of people did I have around? How was I coping? Why was Peter so sick? What was I giving him to eat? And then he asked me if I was a lesbian. Was Peter wanted? Did I go and pick up a man in the street? I didn't want to be down on paper as being a lesbian because next thing he'll do is tell the social workers, and they'll come and visit me and decide that as there's no man around, maybe I'm an unsuitable mother. Then there's a possibility that Peter could be put into care.'

We asked if she had any foundation for this fear; did she know of any instances, apart from custody cases, where children had been taken away and put into care simply because the mothers were lesbians? 'No,' she replied, 'but just because you don't hear about cases doesn't mean it's not happening.' Then why should she be so afraid? 'Because the doctor asked my friend, "Do you know this woman? Are there lesbians in that house?" That was after I'd left the room. He then said, "I suspect Peter is being battered in that house." He obviously associated lesbians with child-battering.' Her friend Amy went on, 'The implication was, because we were lesbian, we didn't want the kid; he was going to be in the way. It was very scary, the doctor coming around – especially because when you want the doctor to come when the child is sick, they don't come. If they knew you were a lesbian, they might decide in some way that you're unfit. It may not be written in the law that they can take your child away, but they can think of something – like this bruise, this burn . . . and that you're a lesbian.'

Rachel and Amy freely admitted that they had no real evidence on which to base their fears. Either, then, they suffer from paranoid fantasies, or the prejudices which lesbians – and particularly lesbian mothers – experience in their contacts with institutionalized authority are deeply threatening and need to be avoided whenever and however possible. The experience of lesbian mothers in the divorce courts clearly reveals that these women have good grounds for believing that authority is prejudiced against them. At the same time it is essential that lesbian mothers involved in fighting for legal custody of their children find ways to confront the assumptions made about them and to negate them if they can.

The story of Sheila demonstrates only too clearly what these women have to face:

'When I first left I took Patrick with me and he lived with my lover, Alice, and me for two years. Meantime I got divorced and my husband married somebody else. He had access all that while on an every other weekend basis. Then he said he wanted the child to go and live with him. We said Patrick was quite happy where he was, he was five years old and we wanted him to stay with us. So my husband said he was definitely going to take us to court. We went to London to fight it in the High Court because we thought we would have a better selection of judges and better solicitors in London. Really we left no stone unturned with the case. We had every member, I think, of Alice's family come along and vouch for us, and mine too. My husband and his wife didn't have anybody to come along and vouch for them. In fact, virtually, they just went to court and said "We're heterosexual and aren't we lovely?" And the judge said, "Yeah, you are lovely."

'Psychiatrists dragged up evidence about prostitutes' children and how they turned out. The whole thing was based on conjecture. Patrick might do this, he might suffer that. Or when he goes to school, how's he going to cope with teasing? Our psychiatrist said he'll cope better if he's living in the household involved, than with the other people. So when he comes home from school to the house and says someone said, "Your mum's a lesbian," they're not going to explain to him the same way I would. Obviously they're not. So our psychiatrist said it would be better for Patrick to be with us and have a proper explanation. But then in the final winding-up the judge said that if Patrick was living with them then he could, for all the world to know, live with a perfectly normal couple and that no one need ever know. Those were his very words : "No one need ever know about his mother's deviation."

'We sat night after night discussing every aspect; if they said this, we would say that. One of the questions that came up was, "Did we have any gay friends?" You can't help but be defensive in a thing like this. We said no, not particularly, but Patrick had obviously said at some stage or other that we had been to Bristol when the National Lesbian Conference was on and they had obviously found out that that's what we went to. We said that that was the only thing we had ever been to and we wouldn't go to a thing like that again and we sold ourselves on that particular issue. I felt quite bad about that. I would have liked to have got up and said, "Yeah, we have plenty of lesbian friends and we're not afraid of the fact and we're not ashamed of the fact." It's difficult, though, because you do feel you're fighting such a big battle. I think really what we tried to say to the court was we're just like any other bod except that we happen to be two women instead of a male and a female. They said we couldn't possibly be lesbians, in fact, because lesbians were known not to love children. So the very fact that we had gone along there to fight for my little boy showed that we must be bisexual, and the fact that we had both had heterosexual relationships before went further to prove that that was possible and if we were bisexual then there was less chance of our being a stable couple!

'The man psychiatrist asked me, when I went to visit him, "In what direction would you encourage the little boy's sexual orientation when he grows up?" I said, "I'm not very sure that you could encourage anybody's sexual orientation in any particular direction, but I think, given that you could, I would encourage him to be heterosexual, because it's easier to be accepted and get on in the world if you're a heterosexual." I distinctly remember that was my answer, because he said to me, "So it's all right for you to be homosexual, but you wouldn't let him be one." In his report he put that I had said I'd encourage Patrick to be homosexual when he grew up. I remember thinking at the time, "Well, I can't win, because if I say I'd encourage him to be homosexual, that will be wrong and if I say heterosexual I will be equally wrong." '

Alice commented, 'When in court I was made aware by society really that I haven't got a title – by people all round; people who were on our side and people who were on their side. I think this is always the case in a lesbian relationship, particularly in our case; i.e., I'm not Patrick's step-mummy. I'm not Patrick's daddy, not his step-daddy. I'm Alice. That's sufficient for me and Patrick. I resented questions like "What appliances do you use?" ' Here Sheila broke in, 'Never in the world would they have asked a heterosexual couple in a custody case the sort of questions they asked us – like "How do you regard each other in front of the child?" There was an unwarranted intrusion into our private life that any heterosexual couple would have been outraged by. I think probably the outcome was decided before we even opened our mouths.'

Sheila's husband was granted custody, care and control. Sheila had access every other weekend and half of the school holidays.

'At Christmas Patrick came to us as agreed by the court, from the 23rd of December to the 30th of December. Now my ex-husband's new wife has just produced a baby boy. So he refused to bring my little boy to the half-way meeting point during the half-term access which has just gone by. We didn't, in fact, have him for half-term and we didn't have him last weekend when we were due to. My ex-husband said his wife was suffering from depression following the birth of the baby. Access hasn't worked very well so far. My little boy went to live with his father in August last year. The first access weekend was in September. That went all right. The following one my ex-husband said they hadn't got enough money to pay for the petrol to bring Patrick to the half-way meeting point. So we got in touch with the solicitor who booked us to go into court again. I spoke to my ex-husband once again about the whole job. I told him that we'd be going back to court if we didn't come to some arrangement. On another occasion he said his windscreen-wiper motor had broken down and he didn't know whether he was going to be able to bring Patrick. We always seem to have the last-minute things – we never know till the last moment whether or not it's all going to work out all right. Every weekend he says we will have to wait to see if anything has happened about the baby. So we haven't been able to make any plans because we never know when the fortnightly access might change round.

'One weekend, just recently, we went to feed our birds, some ducks we have on the lake. Patrick asked if he could do something else. I can't remember what it was, but I said, "I'm sorry, but there isn't enough time to do that, because we've got to set out to meet Daddy." He shot back to our cottage and hid under the bed and we had quite a job to get him out. He said he didn't want to go back to his father. It is very difficult to deal with those sorts of circumstances because one feels extremely tempted to say, "Well, all right, you don't have to. We'll do a bunk with you," or something like that. We do try to persuade him that all is well. You're acting as a double person, because you don't really believe in what you're saying to him. Access I find difficult to contend with – it's like opening a wound every time he comes. A month ago I was pleased and relieved when he'd gone back. It's a horrible thing to say, really, but it's so upsetting. And he's always so happy here and I've never been happier except that I'd really like my child back. That's all I want. I don't see how it can ever be, but we were a family and now we're not any more.'

Sheila has not given up hope, but she accepts that she must

face the possibility of having an estranged son. Like Lilian, she has never had any other feelings but that a lesbian relationship is natural and good for her. In the end, although all the legal decisions had been in his favour, Lilian's husband, ironically, asked to be released from the responsibility of caring for his two sons and returned them to her. At the moment, this is only a remote possibility for Sheila, but one that she can cling to in the most painful moments of separation from her son. Legal opinion in both these cases focused on the fact that these children were boys, for whom it was thought especially important that they had an adult male with whom to identify and on whom to model themselves. We turn next, therefore, to a mother with two daughters, in order to see if the assumptions were any different.

Sylvia lives with her lover, Kirstin, her two daughters Simone, aged eleven, and Nancy, aged eight, together with a rabbit, hamster and cat. It is a lively household; they have a modern house on an estate in the south of England, but when we visited it was nearly empty of furniture, Sylvia's husband having recently removed it. We asked Sylvia how long she had been married and what sort of marriage it had been. 'I've been married for twelve years,' she said. 'It hasn't been exactly a happy marriage. My husband was ill for the last five years. I'd have probably made the break sooner had it not been for his illness, because he was totally dependent on me for a lot of the time. Last summer I reached full consciousness that I couldn't go on living this lie, and having clandestine relationships, which I'd had from a very early age. They were non-physical ones before I got married, but nonetheless I had these feelings. I went to a lesbian conference last summer, still, technically, a happily married woman. I found it a very exhilarating experience and met some very interesting people. I met other mothers at the conference and that gave me the confidence to make the break. At least there were others out there – they did exist. I am economically independent. I have my own house. He had a flat in London, which meant making the break was a lot easier than it is for most lesbian mothers. I am also secure in a job.

'I didn't expect his reaction over the children, that he would want to have the children. We discussed it and each of us wanted the children. I went to a feminist solicitor who told me there was little hope of a lesbian getting custody of the children, although, being financially independent, I might stand a chance. I wasn't living with anyone, so we settled out of court that the children would live with their father, and what seemed at the time excellent arrangements for me. I would have them every other weekend and half the school holidays. So the divorce went to court and the judge agreed these arrangements; he said, "They are not satisfactory, but they are the best under the circumstances." I asked him to define and record the access on the child settlement, but he didn't. He just entered "reasonable access". At the moment, the situation seems to be that provided I'm a good girl and behave myself and my husband approves of whatever relationship I'm in, all is fine. But if he doesn't approve the relationship I'm in, or he feels the children are being adversely affected, he has already said things like "We will have to reconsider the access arrangements." '

We asked Sylvia what she honestly thought her husband's motives were in wanting the children. 'In all honesty,' she replied, 'he really believes it is best for the children to be with him, because he can offer more stability and security.' Had he married again? 'No,' she said, 'he's employing a housekeeper and he has bought a house.' We wondered whether she meant that he could offer more material comfort. 'No, emotional,' she responded. 'The word he uses is that lesbianism is a perversion.' We asked if he had ever said that she had been a bad mother and she said he had not said so before she told him about her lesbianism, but that since then he has said that she was a bad mother all through the marriage. 'He has custody, care and control,' she said, but that she thought she ought to have some, if not all, of these rights and that she had not signed any papers agreeing that her husband should have them.

Sylvia's daughters were playing in the room while we talked to her and we asked the elder, Simone, where she wanted to live. 'Here,' she answered, 'and Nancy does too.' Apparently they had not been asked where they wanted to live, even by their father. We asked whether she would tell him, if he asked, and she said, 'No.' Why not? 'I'm scared of him,' she answered immediately, 'I don't know what he'd say.' Her mother broke in,

'He's very different from me. His attitude is to hide everything behind the curtains.' Would he talk to us, we wondered. 'No,' she answered, 'he wouldn't do it.'

We then enquired in more detail into Sylvia's story. Presumably she had used a solicitor for the out-of-court settlement? Wasn't it rather surprising, therefore, that the solicitor had let care, control and custody go all to one party? 'Well,' she responded, 'I went to a solicitor up to a certain point. When I got the first bill from the solicitor, I was absolutely amazed. It was a bit of a struggle to keep all the bills paid. So I stopped seeing the solicitor, as my husband and I had reached an agreement and he was being reasonable. So by the time we got to court, it was between his solicitor and me, as an individual. On the other hand, am I not right in thinking that all custody arrangements as such, can be started all over again, and, in this instance, I would be eligible for legal aid? I would say, now, to any woman, fight all the way.'

Sylvia, like Lilian and Sheila, is happier as a lesbian than she was as a wife. She told us how particularly deadening the wifely role had been for her. 'I was terribly frustrated. But for years I'd stopped thinking. The daily grind was that you got up in the morning, looked after the children, left them with the nanny; you did some of the housework because you thought the load was too much for her, you went to work, you came home exhausted, you played with the children, you read to them, you put them to bed, you then sat down and ate a meal. You just didn't think – you didn't have time. I was so exhausted by the time I went to bed, I couldn't think constructively about our sexual relationship – to take the initiative – I was just too tired.'

We pointed out that a lot of mothers have the experience, after having a baby, and if they're working, that they're too tired for sex. We wondered if that had been true for her. She said that it had. We asked if her husband had been understanding. 'No,' she replied. 'I don't remember one occasion during our marriage, even up to the end, when I said, "No, I'm tired," or "I've got a headache," that there wasn't an argument about it. It got to the point where it was easier – it would take five minutes – if I accepted it. If I didn't, it would be two hours of argument and I had to accept it in the end. That's the way it went on.'

We asked Sylvia whether she experienced any conflict between being a mother and being a lesbian. 'There is for me now,' she said, 'because I have to divide my time between the two children and Kirstin. I've only had two relationships they've actually seen. I'm talking about lovers. The first one wasn't living here. When she came, she brought her daughter. It was very regulated. We got up before the children, not because we had to, but because it seemed the right thing to do. We were always doing things. But with Kirstin, it all happened so quickly. I've had to form my relationship with her alongside my relationship with the children. So there've been times, from my point of view, when I've wanted to be with her, but there's been "Mummy, can we go swimming?"; "Mummy, can we do this?"; "Mummy can we do that?" '

The girls, who had been in the room all the time, were suddenly interested. 'You should love us more than Kirstin,' Nancy asserted. Her mother responded, 'I love you in a different way to the way I love Kirstin.' Nancy was not mollified. 'You spend more time with Kirstin than you do us.' 'No I don't,' Sylvia replied. 'A lot of the time I spend with Kirstin is with you as well.' We then asked Nancy whether her mother had spent more time with them when their father had been living there. 'No,' Nancy said, 'she was often sleeping on the settee.' Was she looking forward to going to live with her father? 'No,' she told us, it would be 'terrible, terrible'. Why? we asked. 'I don't really want to leave Mummy,' she said.

Returning to Sylvia, we wondered whether there had been less stress with her first lover because she had also been a mother. 'There was less time,' Sylvia replied. 'She was very active politically. I got terribly frustrated because I couldn't see her weekdays, because she was out at this and that. Kirstin said, "I'm going to live with you and move five hundred miles, or whatever, away from home." She's been here all the time, and it feels more like home now she's come.'

'I call myself lesbian,' Sylvia said, 'yet I'm sure it will be levelled against me that I'm bisexual. But I am able now to show more affection in front of the children and more love, far more freely than I ever did in my heterosexual relationship. I feel so much more at one with her. I loved my husband. I still love my husband, in the way one would love a brother. I loved him then as one would love a brother. I'm freed now of this concealed guilt about my emotions.' Part of Sylvia's relief came from this feeling of honesty, but part, also, came from her escape from the wifely role which she had previously found so destructive. 'We share the chores,' she told us. 'Whoever is late in the bath in the morning, the other one does the hoovering. Whoever has the idea for cooking the meal, cooks the meal. We don't have any set roles. And nobody could be said to be the male or the female partner in the relationship.'

We put it to Sylvia and Kirstin that many people say lesbians ought not to have children, because of the possibility of damaging them in some way. 'Out there,' replied Sylvia, 'they see lesbians as desperately seeking a large cock which will change their lives, or a "diesel" on a motorbike who'd really rather be a man.' And Kirstin added, 'I should really be an old veterinary surgeon in her fifties, who lives in the Pennines, breeds dogs, takes Sunday constitutionals, walks with a shooting stick, wears brogues and sensible shoes, a smart jacket and skirt in a dog-tooth tweed, a deer-stalker with fishing feathers on the side, and goes on walking holidays in the Tyrol every year!'

Would Sylvia mind if either or both of her daughters turned out to be lesbians? 'I would be quite happy,' she said. Would she think she had caused it? 'No,' she answered, 'because I'm a product of heterosexual parents and actually a very normal heterosexual-parent family. Nothing traumatic happened to me. And I had a very happy and normal childhood.' We pressed the point, suggesting that many people say that lesbian relationships don't last. 'I'd like to say to that,' Sylvia responded, 'that in the past most homosexual relationships have been closeted. There haven't been the normal family ties – parents, cousins, sisters, brothers, uncles, aunts, nieces, nephews – to give you this sense of permanence; and now you've got this new sort of lesbian: the uncloseted lesbian, the lesbian who keeps a bank manager in her cupboard, not another lesbian. Now we have supportive friends, work and family, who support us. I have now the equivalent of a Jewish mother-in-law who, I hope, if ever Kirstin left me and went back north, would give her a good meal, a good night's sleep, and send her back again. I know that's what my mother would do. And this is what happens in heterosexual families. In the past, we were one or two against the world, but now let's hope that the new opening up of relationships can mean we have this extended support.'

In Sylvia's custody dealings, which are not yet over, no one so far has mentioned the sex of the children as a factor to be taken into consideration with respect to the children's psychlogical development in the same way as it was suggested to be very important in the cases where lesbians had sons. The implication seems to be that it is more urgent for a boy to have a male role model than it is for a girl to know what men are like. The faulty reasoning of this is obvious to anyone with an unbiased eye, since if boys need to know about masculinity at close quarters, so also do girls, especially if the assumption is that they must grow up to marry a man. It would also be logical, if this argument is correct, to remove the sons of any single mothers – widows, divorcées and the unmarried – and place them with male role models. This is not, however, present social policy. It seems that it is not the single mother who is thought unsuitable for the rearing of boys, but the lesbian mother. What sons have to say about this we shall come to later on; here we should simply like to point out that the authorities seem to be more protective of the developing male ego than of the female. We wonder why this should be the case.

Next we can consider a story with a more positive outcome. When we met them, Martha and Selina were jubilant after finally winning a four-year battle for care, control and custody of Selina's three children, two girls and a boy, aged nine, six and seven respectively.

They had been friends since they were thirteen-year-old girls at the same school. Selina got married at twenty-one, but they kept in touch by letter. During that time, Martha had several lesbian relationships. After her third child, a daughter, was born, Selina became very ill. Her marriage was an unhappy one. She phoned Martha and stayed a week with her to recuperate. They became lovers. She returned home, but they kept meeting.

Initially, Selina's husband was friendly and would visit Martha and her mother on his way home through London, but when he heard about their relationship he became increasingly violent. After two years Selina couldn't bear the separation from Martha any longer, nor could she bear being knocked about by her husband.

'In May 1975 I started divorce proceedings on the grounds of irretrievable breakdown. We were still living under the same roof of our council house (in his name). We went to court in September 1976. I was in a nervous state and wanted to stay with Martha for the divorce in a fortnight's time. I had been very depressed and was under the doctor, who said I needed a holiday. I went to the welfare authorities who said they could take the two youngest kids into interim voluntary care for two weeks, so I could have a break to get myself together. The social worker fetched the kids in his car and brought them back after the court case. We then went to court and I got care, custody and control of the children. We came out of court and I said to Martha, "I can't believe it's all gone." We came back to Martha's North London council flat and told her mum, "It's all done." Then the phone rang. It was my solicitor. He said when he got back to his office he had found a message that my husband was contesting the custody because I had put the children in care and because of the lesbian aspect. It dropped like a bombshell. My husband wasn't in court when I got the nisi. Anyway, the solicitor wanted to see me, so we both went.' Martha added, 'The solicitor said a perjury charge was coming up because Selina's counsel said she'd misled him and the court by not telling him that the children were in care.'

'Which wasn't true,' Selina broke in. 'Because when I met my solicitor and counsel before we had to go to court, I asked, "How do I answer – you know, the god thing that sits there – how do I address it?" He said, "You look at her and answer the questions she asks." She asked, "Are the children healthy?" I said, "Yes." "Are they well?" I said, "Yes." She didn't say to me, "Are they at this very moment in time living with you?" Anyway, I *had* told counsel and my solicitor they were in holiday care for only a fortnight. I hadn't told them about the lesbian aspect. I just wanted the divorce to go through as irretrievable breakdown – which is what it was. Then the two letters arrived at my solicitor's, which was the first I knew of it. My husband had disappeared for three months. I didn't know where he'd gone. He hadn't packed his bags. Then he came back to pack and leave for good. Martha had written a letter to me and I answered it, but didn't post it; I wrote to her at the stage when I couldn't stand any more. I felt, God, I can't stand the kids; it wasn't worth being away from her; I'd sooner leave the kids, give up everything; I couldn't see an end to it. I was very depressed. He searched for these letters and took them.

'So we went back to court in December 1976 but Martha wasn't allowed in court. My husband was there. Then I had to answer the perjury bits. Actually it was not perjury, more that I had misled the court. I said, no – I hadn't. I'd just answered the questions as they were put to me; the question was never asked; also I had told my solicitor the children were on holiday. There was heavy breathing and grunts because my solicitor tried to make me say I hadn't told him. Then [referring to the letter to Martha] the judge asked, "Do you still feel that way?" I said, "No, not now." She said, "Did you feel that way?" I said, "Obviously, or I wouldn't have written it then, if I didn't." It was pretty sickening, really. I had to stand up in court and there it was in black and white. She asked, "Is it a lesbian relationship?" Did we make love? Did we – whatever the word is they use? I said, "Yes." I kept saying "Yes". Then she asked, "Do you sleep together?" I said, "Yes." She said, "Do you indulge in a lesbian liaison?" I said, "Yes." By this time I was feeling quite sick and hot under the collar. I kept thinking, I'm not to look ashamed. I had to sit down; I felt quite faint. She brought me a drink. I'm there trying to think – "No, you're not to sort of sleep. You've got to keep your head up. You've got to keep your eyes wide open. You've got to look them in the face" – otherwise I thought I'd feel ashamed. Like anybody, you don't want your private things and love letters all dragged out in court. The judge kept humming and mumbling, "I don't know, I think the best thing is to take these children into care." Bearing in mind that they were that much younger [six, four and three], she really, really wanted those children into care. My husband said I didn't feed them; that they ran around the streets. We'd gone unprepared. We had a different counsel who didn't know anything. I talked with him half an hour before. So he gets up and says, "Your Honour, you do understand we can't act for this client any more." The judge was still concerned about the children; so she calls into court the welfare officer to do a report on the kids. We adjourned until after lunch. I don't know what he did – who he rang – but when we got back, the court welfare officer said these children were being looked after; they were clean; they were fed. Therefore interim care and control should go to me. There I was without counsel or a solicitor. By this time it was all above my head. All I could see was that my children were going into care. In the end I got all three children under the supervision of the County Council. I didn't get the absolute, which normally comes through in six weeks. Now it froze.'

Selina returned to Surrey and stayed there with the children. 'I went to see another solicitor – any solicitor. At that time I thought all solicitors were the same. This one was right snooty with a pin-stripe suit and fat and looked down his nose. He said he would take the case and would I sign something, so that he could get all the papers from the other solicitor and for legal aid. When I saw him again he asked, "Was this right – did we have sex? Did we sleep together?" – all the time looking down his nose. He made me feel sick. He certainly didn't make me feel he'd done me any good.'

A week later, Selina's solicitor sent her a copy of the welfare report ordered by the court. It distressed Martha and Selina greatly, because it twisted everything they had said. They recalled that the social worker had phoned and asked them to call at his office near Selina's home. He asked Martha, indirectly, if she looked at the children with the idea that she could be their father. Was she maintaining them? How much did she earn in the factory? He commented that she earned more than he did. He knew Selina was on Social Security and that she received no maintenance at that time (or ever did, in fact). He asked Selina if she was sexually satisfied by Martha. Did she reach orgasm? Did they both reach orgasm? Did they enjoy it? He reassured them that he knew two women friends, one of whom wore a tie, waist coat and shirt and dressed like a man when they went out together. Selina and Martha denied the more preposterous insinuations and answered the sex questions honestly. Neither the home situation nor the children were mentioned, nor was any request made to see them.

'In the report,' Selina told us, 'he said we reached orgasm by mutual masturbation. He said I was a liar and manipulated the situation in order to con everybody. That I wasn't and had never been ill. That Martha and I were an evil influence on the kids. That the deviation was all hers. The only time he mentioned the kids was to recommend that they be put into care. What's more, he was the social worker who collected them and brought them back after their fortnight's holiday. So he knew how they were looked after and what the house was like. So I went bowling over to this snotty solicitor with the report. This social worker couldn't be found. He vanished off the face of the earth. The solicitor kept saying, "Don't worry, we can sort all that out in court." ' Martha added, 'The report also said the children had been *put* into care twice. The first time was *holiday* care. The second time was *voluntary* care. It was a dreadful report. It was all lies.'

'But the judge reads this,' Selina explained. 'They have nothing else to go on to decide. I kept saying to this solicitor that the social worker never went to see the children. He never mentioned that he'd visited my home fetching and returning the kids; that we'd never used words like "mutual masturbation". The solicitor says, "We'll sort that out in court." Well, I'm nearly going off my head. To my mind it was like going to war with empty guns. You don't do this. You answer it all. You work it out in front of it all. So whatever you get thrown at you, you can answer it all. Then I come back and we go to Martha's social worker with the report. He's furious. He can't believe it. He gives us the number of MIND and Ron Lacey. We rang and he said, "Come over." He read the report and said he'd never seen anything like it in his life. He then gave me the number of solicitors called Offenbach. We came home and rang them.'

Selina and Martha met Tessa Lindop at Offenbach's in April 1977 with the court case coming up in June. It is worth mentioning at this stage that the divorce was at the nisi stage. Selina had interim care and control with a welfare supervision on both her and the children. Proceedings had dragged on since May 1975. During this time there had been much to-ing and fro-ing between the two women, solicitors, social workers and welfare authorities, with visits to the children in care every weekend and summonses to court. Selina and Martha had no knowledge of lesbian support groups, gay switchboards, counselling or advice. They knew no other lesbians.

Tessa suggested going to court in June to ask for an adjournment, to give them time to collect all the papers, to fill the cavernous holes in their defence. Meanwhile, Selina's husband had himself asked for an adjournment, so they didn't go to court until September, when they appeared in front of the same woman judge. Selina's husband, his solicitor and counsel were present. Selina's counsel, Maggie Rae, pleaded that the social worker who made the report should be present to answer to everything he had written and asked for a subpoena if necessary. The social worker couldn't be found and was not present to answer to his report. Selina was given her absolute as her husband submitted that he had formed a relation with a Miss S., whom he intended to marry, after which he would apply for custody of the three children. Meanwhile he wanted them to go into care. Selina's counsel pleaded that he was living in the family home, not with *Miss* S., but with *Mrs* S., who had been divorced previously by Mr B. She had two children. The younger, aged ten, was living with her current husband, Mr S., who was in the process of divorcing her – and there were two lodgers in the family home. This was the *real* reason why Selina's husband couldn't provide a home and wanted the children to go into care. Selina's counsel went on to say that Selina's husband constantly beat her up and the doctor's letter in evidence was available. So the case was adjourned for another welfare report.

In December 1977 Selina made herself homeless and was allocated to a half-way hostel in the depths of the country. She had two bedrooms, and use of a kitchen and bathroom. The other five bedrooms in the hostel were empty. She and her children were the only inhabitants besides the caretaker.

'I must say one thing,' Selina commented. 'I do think it is relevant. I do think people should know how far the Welfare can go. When you've got kids in voluntary care, the Welfare can do nothing when you want to take your children for the weekend – for a holiday – take them out of care. You've not relinquished any rights by putting your kids into voluntary care. Social workers go on the fact that you don't know how far they can go. I do believe that if you can answer everything they throw at you, you can keep going. For instance, when I made myself homeless with my eldest daughter, the court questioned it as an irresponsible act. I answered that with, "No." It wasn't. Because it was the only way I could get a home and get all my children back together and the council had to give me accommodation.'

The welfare report ordered by the court in September was done by a director of the local welfare authority, a woman to whom Selina and Martha constantly applied to have the children for weekends and holidays and finally to take out of care. She worked for the same local authority which dealt with Selina's homelessness. This officer also visited Martha's London council flat to see how the children fared there. Eventually, in September 1978, Selina got a council flat of her own with the children in the same area as her original home and still under the jurisdiction of this same welfare officer.

'Tessa kept hanging on and handing it on and dragging it on as long as she could,' explained Selina. ' "The longer the children are back with you, the better," she told me. "For when we go back to court, we can say these children have been back with their mother for such and such a time and there's nothing wrong with them." I felt quite confident with Tessa all the way through. We felt we were battling it together, which we were, for the first time.'

Finally, Selina and Martha were summoned to appear in the Registrar's court in August 1979. They went to see Tessa and a different woman counsel. The welfare report was very good. It concentrated on the children's physical, emotional and psychological well-being. School reports were enclosed. A cool assessment was made of Martha's and Selina's characters. This was backed by a welfare report from Martha's social worker. 'They wanted to know how we were,' Selina went on. 'Were the children happy? Were we happy? Tessa and Joanna, my counsel, were worried that if we mentioned that we slept together, the Registrar might say, "Well, this had better go back to the judge." We said, "We've fought all along that we love each other, that we want to live together, that we will live together." '

Martha, Selina, the children, Tessa, Joanna and the welfare officer all went to the Registrar's court. Selina's husband's solicitor was there. After fifteen minutes it was all over. Selina got custody, care and control. 'It was an anti-climax, after those four years of aggravation, obscenities and upheavals,' said Selina.

The story of Selina and Martha shows only too clearly how a single social worker can wield enormous power over a family's destiny, and how the wrong solicitor can cause havoc to a family and to children's natural attachments to those they love and by whom they are loved and cared for. The trustees of English law are traditionally conservative, but the implicit assumption in all these proceedings, as in many like them which we have not had the space to mention, is that the very existence of a lesbian relationship is, of itself, indicative of bad mothering – indeed, of such extreme bad mothering that children should be in any home available rather than in the mother's. This assumption must properly be described as a prejudice, since no objective evidence, psychiatric, psychological or educational, is cited in support of it. The defence in one lesbian custody case made a strong point of this lack of evidence. Subsequently, with some aid from the Nuffield Foundation, a project was undertaken which sought to compare the psychosexual development of lesbians' children with that of the children of single non-lesbian mothers, since single mothers do not lose custody of their children on grounds of their sexuality. Some people may think that the children of lesbians should be compared with the children of a married couple living together, as that is what is generally considered the norm. But if such a comparison were made, and if any significant differences were found, it would not be clear whether the differences were due to the fact that a man was present in the household, or whether they were due to the sexuality of the mother. In any case, many studies have been done comparing the development of children brought up in one-parent families with that of children in a two-parent, heterosexual household, and such studies have found that where there are disadvantages for single-parent children, they are associated with the much lower level of income which single-parent families have to live on. Risks to healthy emotional and social development, that is, are directly connected to the problems caused by poverty. Comparing lesbian mothers' children, therefore, with the children of heterosexual single mothers, is a way of isolating the factor of the mother's sexuality in order to find out whether it is harmful or indeed even relevant to the healthy development of children.

The project was carried out by Susan Golombok and Ann Spencer, both psychologists, and Michael Rutter, Professor of Child Psychiatry at the Institute of Psychiatry in London. At the time of going to press, the results of this study have not been analysed down to the last detail, but there is so far no evidence to suggest that there are any differences between the two groups of children in psychosexual development or incidence of psychiatric disorder. The study was carried out because of the refusal of courts in Britain and the USA to award custody of their children to lesbian mothers without any empirical evidence to support the claims that children in these circumstances would not be harmfully affected by this experience. Particular concern was expressed about the emotional and psychosexual development.

Susan Golombok explained the project to us as follows: 'Children with lesbian mothers were compared with children having heterosexual mothers. By administering standardized interviews and questionnaires to the mothers and children data were collected concerning the two specific areas of development to be compared. There were twenty-seven lesbian mothers and twenty-seven heterosexual mothers, with thirty-seven children of school age and above in the lesbian mothers group, and thirty-eight children, of school age and above, in the heterosexual mothers group. What we did was to interview the mothers and the children about the family situation, about the work pattern of the mother, about the past and present relationships of the mother, and we also interviewed the mothers about the children's social activities, friends and psychiatric state. The children's interviews concerned their friendships, toys and favourite activities. We then compared the two groups. The main things we were looking at were sex roles and gender identity in the children and their psychiatric state.

'Basically, we found no differences between the two groups of children in their social and emotional development – in both groups their friendships follow fairly similar patterns. There was also no difference in the incidence of psychiatric disorder and the incidence of disorder was no higher than is found generally. With respect to sex role development, there were no differences between the groups.'

These results, which correspond to similar studies done in the United States, suggest that there are no specific risks of emotional disturbance to the children of lesbian mothers. Similarly, the preconception that the psychosexual development of the children of lesbian mothers will differ in significant ways from that of the majority, also seems to be unfounded. Until these kinds of prejudices are supported by objective evidence, the courts and other public authorities should eschew them and instead show impartiality of judgement and evaluation.

A further point here is that judicial authorities arbitrating between two parents contesting custody seem to be unaware that in most cases where the father is asking for custody, it is not he but his new wife who will be bringing up the children. These fathers are generally not willing to take the place of the mother by staying at home, looking after the children and living on Supplementary Benefit. Even if they were willing, social prejudice about the proper places of men and women would make it extremely difficult for them to do so. Welfare authorities are suspicious of such men, assuming that any man wanting to take on 'women's work' might be motivated by 'selfish' desires to shirk 'proper' employment. Why anyone in authority should think a stepmother more able and motivated to bring up children than their own mother, who has even fought for her right to do so, is a problem which should cause not only bafflement but serious concern.

One case in particular, which was brought to our notice, illustrates another anomaly in custody decisions. A lesbian mother lost care, control and custody, but was granted limited access to her two small children in London. After a while the father found the children hampered his working and social life, so he sent them off to the west of England to live with his mother and sister without reference to the court. He visited the children irregularly, perhaps once a month. The distance deprived the mother of any access at all. Her bitterness is surely justified in the knowledge that her children are being brought up in the very situation that disqualified her from gaining custody – a household of two women!

In our discussions with these women a number of other issues emerged. They expressed fear and suspicion of all social authorities – of the judicial system, of social workers, of doctors, of all the machinery of the Welfare State. The most constant fear was that if their lesbianism were officially known, these mothers would lose their children, irrespective of all the other circumstances of their lives, including economic independence. It might be argued by the orthodox that this fear is natural and that there is no onus on the authorities to dispel it, since lesbians have rejected the social norm of heterosexuality and have therefore earned the antipathy of the State, along with criminals, psychopaths and subversives. More careful thought, however, should reveal the more disturbing attitude which lurks behind such a judgement, and that is the awe-inspiring importance given to sexuality in the human matters of family living and child rearing.

In the cases we have described, the following concerns were given only secondary importance: the children's own feelings about their parents and about where they wanted to live; the mothers' nurturing and caring abilities; the mothers' willingness and ability to provide a home; the mothers' economic adequacy; the practical and emotional alternatives offered by the contesting fathers; and the role – domestic and economic – which the lesbian partners of the mothers were willing to play. In the final case, that of Selina and Martha, a welfare officer emerged who was willing to consider these factors. All the other people involved clearly considered the sexual behaviour of the mother to be of enormous, all-consuming importance. This assumption was then systematically projected onto both mother and children – that is, it was assumed that the mother's sexual behaviour would be the all-consuming interest of her own life, and that for her children it would be the all-consuming, definitive fact about their mother. It seems to us that such a degree of obsession with sex-

uality must lead to distortions of judgement in cases where the
lives of young human beings are to be permanently affected by
instruments of the State.

Such attitudes of implicit prejudice, both social and legal,
expressed against lesbian mothers, are international. They are
shown most forcibly in countries where lesbian mothers come
out into the open and fight for their children. It would become
tedious to catalogue every custody case we know of in each
country, since the patterns of prejudice repeat themselves with
remarkable similarity. However, in the United States of America,
the success rate of lesbian mothers awarded custody, care and
control is higher than that in Britain. One case of particular
interest occurred in Denver, Colorado, where the lover of a
deceased lesbian mother was awarded custody of the daughter.
Jeanette Hatzopoulos and Donna Levy lived together for thirteen years and had brought up Betty, Jeanette's daughter, for
the first six years of her life. In 1974 the lesbian couple separated, but Donna continued to see Betty several times a week.
In 1976 Jeanette committed suicide. Her sister and brother-in-
law fought for custody and got a temporary custody decision
provided they sought therapy once a week together with Betty.
They did not do so. Then they announced that they were separating. At this point the judge awarded custody to Donna. Judge
Weeks, a woman, emphasized that Donna's lesbianism should
have nothing to do with the issue. 'Donna's sexual preference
has not affected the child in the past and is not related to her
ability to parent the child,' she said. 'Her strengths as a parent
to the child are her sensitivity, her warmth and her depend-
ability. When sexual preference would become significant to the
child, Donna has the ability to deal with it intelligently, openly
and honestly.'

As well as an exaggerated view of the importance of sexuality
to a lesbian and her children, a corresponding, and perhaps
resultant attitude, was expressed. Amy and Rachel were surprised
and alarmed by the visit of a senior doctor, who asked a great
number of questions about where Rachel had got her baby,
whether she wanted it, and so on. The meaning of these questions
for the two women was the doctor's indirect assumption that
lesbians do not like children and would not want to have any.

The judge in Sheila's case actually expressed this assumption directly, by saying that everyone knew lesbians did not like children. We could not find any evidence, among the mothers we met, to support this view. There are certainly lesbians who do not like children, just as there are heterosexual women, and men, who do not like children. And it is very easy, easier than for a heterosexual woman, for a lesbian who does not like children and does not want to have any, to avoid doing so. But to say that a *mother* will not like her own child simply because she is a lesbian is a serious charge which people in authority should not be permitted to make without very convincing objective evidence to support it. That there is, to date, no such evidence in existence ought to give the authorities cause to reflect and to resist the promulgation of their own prejudices. If they do not, they are not only meddling with the domestic happiness of mothers and children, but they are also encouraging a lack of trust in, and a hostility towards, the machinery of the State itself.

Finally, all the mothers, in whatever country, expressed a deep conviction that, in the unfortunate event of parents contesting guardianship of their child, the primary right belongs with the mother. The father enjoys an equal half of the responsibility for conceiving a child, but the mother has contributed more – she has gone through nine months of pregnancy, through birth, and, in nearly all cases, through most of the tasks and experiences of nurturing. She feels, because of these things, that her right to the child is greater than the right of the father. A recent British judgement gave support to this view, when a judge ruled that a wife had the right to procure an abortion against the wishes of her husband. The husband argued that she should bear the child, since it was as much his right as hers to decide whether the child should be born. Since both parties could not be satisfied, having directly opposing wishes, the judge ruled that the mother had the prior right and with this legal authority she went ahead and had her abortion. If, in such cases, the mother's right is acknowledged to be greater than the father's, it is especially difficult to sympathize with the view that a mother's right will become secondary to the father's if the mother is found to be a lesbian.

There is one ultimate irony; mothers contesting custody cases are not tested for lesbianism and would probably be outraged if they were. Very many, therefore, conceal their lesbianism and receive custody of their children in the usual way, thus reinforcing the hypocrisy of authorities who are not in the least concerned by what they do not know.

4 Where There's a Will, There's a Way

Younger lesbians, who have become aware of their sexual preference at an earlier stage than those who ventured into marriage, and who are familiar with the custody battles fought by divorced lesbian mothers, are increasingly turning away from men and marriage as a means of conceiving children and choosing a new way – artificial insemination by donor, otherwise called AID. For any woman, lesbian or not, who does not want to face the possibility of losing her child either to the child's father or to the State, AID offers an alternative which restores the primary rights and responsibilities to the mother. It offers, too, the possibility of separating the need for sexual relationship from the need for family. And it gives, ironically, the ultimate independence which those in the abortion campaign are still fighting for – a woman's right to choose for herself, and in deference to no man or woman, what she will do with her own fertility.

AID is not against the law in Britain, although it is in some other countries. Nor is it disapproved of by the central ethical committee of the British Medical Association. It is provided on request by the British Pregnancy Advisory Service, by some National Health Service clinics, and by some private gynaecologists. It is also performed by self-help groups of women, with the aid of sympathetic men friends, without the auspices of any medical personnel. More AID babies have been born in Britain than can be calculated, since most are born to infertile marriages where the baby's father is described on the birth certificate, untruthfully, as the mother's husband. Since there is no practicable way for the authorities to determine the actual paternity of every child, a blind eye is turned to this fraud, and such children, although theoretically illegitimate, are made legitimate by their birth certificates. Single mothers who give birth to AID children, like other single mothers where paternity is not acknowledged, enter 'father unknown' on the birth certificate of their children. The married state of the mother is what, in practice, confers legitimacy on the child. This may, to some strange minds, seem a good way of classifying women, but it is clearly a very unjust way of classifying children.

We discussed AID and its relevance for lesbians with two gynaecologists, one who works in a National Health Service clinic and the other in private practice.

Dr James, a clinical and academic gynaecologist, works in the infertility clinic of a large teaching hospital. He told us he had been working and training there for five years and that during that time he had worked with donor insemination. Our first question was whether the technique of artificial insemination was a complicated one. He replied that it was not, that it was, in fact, 'terribly simple', but even so it was not part of general medical training. 'It is just a different way of getting a sperm to meet an egg. It happens to be an anonymous sperm, instead of a sperm labelled, as it were, by name. When people think it through, they get rid of a lot of negative feelings. The important thing is that genetically, fifty per cent of this baby is an unknown quantity. On the other hand, the person you know and love so much is equally, genetically, an unknown quantity. AID is really a human ethical issue, more than a medical one. The actual medical side of it is very simple. Donor insemination is actually in the medical field purely because it arose out of investigations of people who were having difficulty falling pregnant for reasons unknown. Therefore you had to do a lot of tests. I feel, personally, that this is in a way a little bit like termination of pregnancy. It's not surprising that the technique should have originated in medical hands. That is not an argument – *per se* – for it remaining in medical hands.' Most of Dr James' experience with AID, therefore, has been with infertile marriages.

Dr Smith is a gynaecologist in private practice, rather than research, but his theoretical approach was similar to that of Dr James. 'AID was done for those who had complained of infertility. So they were examined and investigated,' said Dr Smith. 'Initially, because of being unsure of what was going on with lesbian couples, I went through the same procedure as I would for somebody who was infertile. Then I asked myself, "Why am I doing this examination?" I hadn't met lesbians as lesbians. I didn't know much about them. I thought: "Here is a young healthy woman who wants AID. Yet I am treating her as if she were an infertile woman." I don't think one should use every opportunity at any contact with a patient to do a complete check-up. If a woman's menstrual history is normal and she doesn't have any symptoms, then I would expect her to have no abnormality. Unless time was going by and she wasn't getting pregnant. Then I would examine her in the same way as I would a married person. That was my attitude after the first two or three lesbians who came to me for AID.'

There is clearly, then, a difference in motivation among women wanting AID. The original, and most common, reason is the infertility of a marriage, either because the husband is infertile or because the particular combination of husband and wife mitigates against a pregnancy. The other reason, one that has emerged more recently and the one particular to lesbians, is the desire to achieve pregnancy without the complications of marriage or the unpleasantness of casual heterosexual encounters. Women who want AID for this second reason are assumed to be as normal and healthy as any other intending mothers and therefore not to need any specifically medical techniques to help them to become pregnant. We asked Dr Smith what procedures he used for his intending lesbian mothers.

There are two main considerations. First, the selection of the donor, and second, the best time of the month for the insemination. Dr Smith explained that the donor must be healthy. 'He's got to be free of disease as far as you can ascertain. He's got to be in a position to father a child. You save the woman a lot of time hanging around waiting to get pregnant by making sure that the semen is sound. It is very important to have a history. Most donors who volunteer are motivated and they wouldn't want to cause infection. For the record, we do a blood test, principally to satisfy ourselves. I explain to them that, on this particular day, there's no infection, but I don't want to keep repeating the blood test every time they give semen and I rely on them to tell me if there is the slightest risk of infection. We've got to depend on that. For the sperm I do a microscope test. I want to see sufficient quantity, numbers, sufficient percentage of motile sperms. Any technician can do this. I like to see the donor to talk to him. That gives me more information. I satisfy myself that this is a good donor, rather than just leave it to a laboratory technician. I chat to the donor. I ask what they're doing and their family background, their medical history.'

What did he mean by a 'good donor'? 'I mean good and healthy,' he replied. 'A good family history. I would like to have somebody who has already sired a child, but we don't exclude those who haven't because we can prove very soon that they are capable. It would be nice to know that he's produced healthy children before, therefore married men would be ideal. But married men don't always come forward, for various reasons.'

We then asked how the specimen of semen is produced. 'By simple masturbation,' he told us. 'There's no other way of getting it. Even with bulls, they have to masturbate them. Semen is the fluid, sperms are the little things that swim around in the fluid. Only one sperm is needed to fertilize. I use fresh semen, as opposed to frozen semen, it's convenient.'

In Dr James' National Health Service clinic the procedures for donor selection and semen collection are similar. The donors are 'young people, often students, who don't have offspring, who appear to be fit, healthy and don't have any family history of any diseases we know are likely to be inherited. We ask them,' Dr James told us. 'We don't check back through their medical records. Of course, being medical students, they're pretty conscious of family medical history. It would be nice to know that the donor had had normal offspring. We do look at their chromosomes to see that they are normal. Plus a blood test and sperm count, of course, and perhaps a urine test. We call up the donors, as and when we need them, and ask them to abstain from sex for a few days. They produce a sample by masturbation into a container. That's fairly important, actually, that it is by masturbation, and directly into the sterile container, from which we actually take the sperms. We mix them with a chemical which helps storage. A lot of people find it easier to masturbate into a sheath or to produce a sample by intercourse into a sheath and then pour it out. The chemicals in a sheath are bad news as far as reproduction is concerned. Nowadays, some sheaths have spermicide in them, but even before that the lubricants slightly damaged the sperms. When the sperms are produced in the testes, they come out into a very tiny wiggly little tube. It's only when they get to the root of the penis and come up past the little glands called seminal vesicles that they get fluid attached to them. Nobody knows too much about that fluid and its exact relevance for producing a pregnancy, but there's no doubt that it's crucial and that it contains food for the sperms to last them on their journey, besides giving them something to swim in. Sperms extracted directly from the testes would be infertile. Most places doing donor insemination like to use frozen sperm samples because it is easier for the timing. If you've got your samples there all the time and you've got your lady who's only able to fall pregnant at a certain time of the month, it's easier that way. That's where the specialist bit comes in. Freezing and thawing the sperm is quite specialized. If that isn't done properly, you get very poor results. It's a question of freezing and keeping sperm in liquid nitrogen. You have to pay a certain amount for liquid nitrogen top-ups. The main cost is the canister, which is something like $230. The costs are staffing costs and getting the sperms. We pay the donor's expenses.'

We asked whether there was much difference in the conception chances between using fresh or frozen semen. 'It makes little difference,' he replied. 'Even with the best freezing techniques, you will lose about fifteen per cent of the mobile sperms.' If there were no bureaucratic or timing problems, wouldn't they prefer to use fresh semen? 'Yes,' he said. 'I think the timing problems are the crucial ones.' If fresh semen is used what is the longest time they can remain viable? 'I'm not sure how long you could keep them for,' he said. 'We know that in nature sperms can be found around maybe sixty hours after initial intercourse. The motility certainly drops drastically after a couple of hours. In practice, we always use them within an hour. But certainly you could go a bit longer than that.'

We wondered whether the clinic ever used mixed samples, or whether mother 'A' always had the sperm of donor '5'. 'The people who run the clinic don't know who the donors are,' Dr

James told us. 'What we have is a book of numbers and corresponding characteristics. If we don't have number 5, who is that lady's usual donor, we pick another one who is similar. We never give a mixed sample. But, from one month to another, we may change donors, according to availability. A technique which people have used is to mix in a little of the husband's semen at the time of the insemination, for psychological reasons. There are probably medical disadvantages in this because it wasn't designed for two different people's sperms to be together. They probably inhibit one another. Donors can supply specimens as often as is reasonable. To get good specimens, ideally, the donors should abstain from orgasm for three or four days before, because then they get a higher sperm count. But I would be very surprised if our donors practise this. They are all healthy young men and in the main, medical students.'

Dr Smith also said that donors could be used as often as practicable. 'Unlike donating blood,' he said, 'you can use a donor as often as he's prepared to be used. As you know, a bull is used many, many times with one ejaculation. A very small amount is needed. They put it in a little tube and divide it up among very many cows. As I don't have that many recipients, I don't need to divide the semen into so many parts.'

From the donor's side, then, the procedure is very simple. He should be healthy, which is ascertained, in practical terms, by asking his medical history. He needs to be fertile, which is most quickly ascertained by taking a sperm count or by his having already fathered offspring. For self-help groups, who do not use a doctor and who do not have a microscope, donors who have not achieved a pregnancy within an agreed time period can be dropped by mutual consent. With these factors established, the donor has simply to masturbate into a sterile container at the time he is asked to do so. In large clinics, his semen is frozen and stored; in small practices or self-help groups, the fresh semen is inseminated within an hour.

The second important part of the procedure is the mother's. She is asked to keep a temperature record, which means taking her temperature with an ordinary thermometer each morning, before she gets out of bed, before smoking, drinking tea or going to the toilet – as soon as possible, that is, after she has woken up.

Each morning she plots this temperature on a graph, so that after two or three months the times of her ovulation can be clearly seen. 'If a woman's period is regular,' Dr Smith explained, 'every twenty-eight days, then you assume that she ovulates on the fourteenth day, counting the first day of her period as the first day. If the cycle is not so regular – for instance, she has her period regularly every twenty-six days – then you count it on the twelfth day, but you don't know when she's going to start the next period. So in that case you keep a temperature record and the temperature goes up when she ovulates and you get a fair idea. Now, you *might* miss it, as you're waiting for the temperature to go up, but you get a fair idea by looking at two or three months. So you do an AID session then, and a couple of days later and then a couple of days after that. I had a nurse who wasn't so regular that she could tell when she ovulated. She suggested five sessions, off her own bat, as she wanted to get pregnant as quickly as possible. So she had five and got pregnant immediately.'

In one self-help group we spoke to, there was an intending mother whose periods were unusually irregular. She kept a temperature chart for three months and decided to begin inseminations in the fourth month as soon as her temperature rose. She then had an insemination for four consecutive days. She conceived immediately but lost the baby at two months, due to spontaneous miscarriage. She repeated the procedure two months after the miscarriage, conceived again and is, at the time of writing, in the fifth month of pregnancy.

The mother's part, therefore, consists in having an insemination as soon as possible at the time when she ovulates, which is most exactly ascertained from her temperature chart. But for a woman with a regular cycle, ovulation can be taken to be on the fourteenth day after her last period has begun. She should then have inseminations, at twenty-four to forty-eight hour intervals, for the next four to five days.

The insemination may be done by the doctor or by any other person. In NHS fertility clinics, it is done by the doctor, who, because he is mostly treating infertility patients, uses a medical technique. Dr James explained: 'All that it actually involves is passing the usual gynaecological speculum, so that you can see the entrance to the womb, and then taking a little straw containing the sperms, attached to a syringe, putting it to the entrance to the womb, and squirting.'

Dr Smith expanded further : 'When a gynaecologist was asked by the press, "Would you yourself inseminate, or let the partner do it?" he replied, " Oh! Of course I'd do it personally. I would never entrust anybody else to do it." By doing it in private practice, personally, gynaecologists are doing this big mystical bit. They use special tools, special instruments and gear. Special tubes. There is a cup with a tube that leads to a syringe. And you're supposed to put the cup against the cervix and inject the semen into the cup so that the cervix dips into the cup and you need to increase the quantity diluted with saline. It's called an inseminating cup. This is used in cases of infertility, where both people are sub-fertile – not infertile – and they want to get the best possible chance. So then I ask myself, "Why should I use the cup with lesbians?" Nature doesn't require this – just plonk the semen into the top end of the vagina. It is not a good procedure to dilate the cervix. It is bad to push the semen into the cervix. I have done that on occasion, in desperation, when I feel with infertile couples there is an antagonism to the sperms in the cervical fluid. I have passed a very, very fine tube into the uterus in order to plant the semen there. It is not a recommended procedure. In fact, it's a procedure that is almost calculated to misfire for several reasons. Sperms seem to require that mucus in the right sort of thickness to climb up. You can't just plonk semen into the uterus and let it make its own way up. It might be irritating the lining of the uterus. I've only used the husband's semen for this particular hurdle of cervical fluid rejection. But it's not the thing I would recommend in ordinary AID. So I asked myself, "Why use special instruments when we're not dealing with an abnormal situation?" My simple answer was that special instruments weren't necessary. Nature doesn't require them so I don't need to do what nature doesn't do.

'I use a 1 ml. diabetic syringe, just because it's the most convenient for implanting the semen at the top of the vagina. It's sterile. It doesn't have to be kept sterile, but if it is sterile it's clean and free of any infection. That's all you really need. It's so easy to use. You draw up the semen out of the container, which can be a pill-container, or an egg-cup. The syringe is thinner than any tampon I've seen. Anybody who can insert a tampon can insert this without any pain. And push the plunger. It doesn't do any damage. There's no needle. It's long enough to reach the end of the vagina. You can use a 2 ml syringe – it's a little wider, but it's shorter. You're taking twice the amount in a shorter length. The 1 ml syringe is seven millimetres thick and three inches long. It's smooth, it's plastic – it's simple. AID shouldn't be painful. When the donor has left the semen, we keep it in a covered container at room temperature. We give the donor warning of the appointment in the hope he will abstain from orgasm for a couple of days before. We can't guarantee this. The semen can go into any sort of container, provided it is sterile : just to guarantee it's free from infection. After the semen's been implanted, it's a good idea to lie on your back with the bottom raised for about twenty minutes – just to prevent leaking. Lesbian women get pregnant quicker than heterosexual women using AID.'

Having established the procedure for AID, we asked the gynaecologists about two other matters : what they thought their donors' motivations were, and what reactions they had to the idea that women whose husbands were not infertile might want AID.

Dr James told us that he was particularly interested in what made men volunteer to donate semen. 'I'm fascinated by it, personally,' he said. 'I think the whole thing that makes people donors, whether it's blood or sperm, is a very interesting topic, but that's the psychiatrist in me. I don't think the motivation matters in the achievement of pregnancy. If they are doing it for the worst motives, they can't be inherited.'

Dr Smith concurred on this point. 'I do ask them,' he said, 'but they don't say anything remarkable. I don't give much credence to a simple answer as to why they've come along. Any more than, "Why do you want to be a doctor?" There isn't a simple answer. It's very difficult to get behind that unless you do a full psychological examination, which I don't propose to do with each person. I don't think it's relevant to our purposes. The fact that he wants to prove himself to himself, as perhaps some of them want to, doesn't particularly bother me. The main thing is that they're healthy and for whatever reason they are prepared to donate their semen. When I have the specimen under the microscope, I let the donor see it. It gives him a bit of interest. He's come a long way. He's volunteered.'

As gynaecologists, then, these practitioners stressed that only the physical health of the donor is of any importance. His motives make no difference to the quality of the genetic material he is contributing. Dr James went into more detail on this point : 'We have a lot of superficial ideas about what effect the outside world has, once baby's there. We have very little information on the formative influence, in the *inside* world, from egg to birth. It has to be important. If we thought that genes were the only important thing, it might create a problem. But at the moment of birth the baby is more of its mother than its father. From that moment on, it's whatever the environment is. Wherever the genes come from becomes really irrelevant. I think that is something people don't often think through. For this reason, I think AID gives a very definite advantage over adoption for those who are thinking over these two alternatives. In regard to the donors themselves, it is important to stress the true blind anonymity. By that I mean the person giving the sperm must not have any idea which sperms belong to which donor. The doctor should know only the number and the characteristics. The donor should never know his number.'

After talking to the gynaecologists we met an AID donor and asked, first, why he had wanted to donate his semen and what his feelings were about it. Henry lives in a council flat in a large city, is thirty-six years old and works with antiques. He volunteered to be a donor after hearing about lesbian women who wanted children. 'I felt very sympathetic towards lesbian mothers,' he explained. 'I felt that I could help them in this way to have children, which otherwise would have been impossible for them. I'm not too worried that I don't know the mother. It's the cause that I think of more than the outcome. You see, all the unmarried mothers who go there, I take to be lesbian. I just assume they are, so I think it really doesn't matter who the mother is. I'm doing it because otherwise I'd just be masturbating. This way I feel I'm helping people who want to be inseminated. I'd reached a stage in my life where I thought I might never get married. I might never sire children. This seemed a good opportunity.'

We asked how he reacted to the knowledge that he had fathered children. 'Well,' he said, 'I'm not quite sure whether I have. I haven't heard, at the moment, but if I knew that I had, it would fill me with a certain satisfaction – that life hadn't been a complete waste, that I had used it for a purpose. I'm rather glad that I'm not getting involved.'

But if he was told that a woman was carrying his child, wouldn't he feel that it was really his? 'I would feel it was her child, rather than my child,' he replied. 'I'm just providing a service.' We asked him if he did it for the money. 'No,' he answered. 'There's not a lot of money involved. The doctor said, "I'm not buying your semen. The money is to cover your expenses." '

Another donor concurred that money was not the object. Edward lives in a flat in north London and is a professional man. He donated semen under different circumstances to Henry. 'I was asked by a woman friend if I would be a donor to a lesbian couple. I was asked about my medical history in great detail. My first thoughts were "What am I doing? What is my responsibility?" Before I agreed to donate I wanted to be assured that the people who wanted the kid really wanted it. So the reply came back that they had one kid of two years and had been trying to get another one and they couldn't. I care about people in relationships. If a child helps a relationship in a situation where, by nature, they can't create a child, then I'm prepared to help that. I am not a breeder. My brother and sister have families, but in no way do I want to have them myself.'

We asked Edward what his feelings were about the parents being lesbian. 'Um . . . what should they have been?' he replied. 'Sure. Why not? This is the same situation had I been confronted by a heterosexual couple who were impotent.'

Edward arranged to meet his friend in his flat at 9.00 am. 'I'd read a manuscript which said it's preferable to have forty-eight hours' abstinence before giving your sperm, so I was very good for two days. My friend arrived with a brown paper parcel.

This was the first setback. I thought I'd get something like a specimen bottle you get in hospital. This was more a test tube. I thought, "Aiming into that, I'm going to lose it all over the carpet or on the sheets," so the tension built up. I lay on the bed with my picture books. I couldn't get an erection. I was sweating. I knew I wasn't going to make it. So I go back to the sitting-room. We had a cup of coffee and chatted for a bit. She was smashing. Then I went back to the bedroom and looked at this test-tube bloody thing. (Why can't they give you something a bit bigger? I'm quite serious about this, because I think it might put men off.) Anyway, I made it using the picture books. There was no problem making it the second and third times.'

Since Edward did not know whether he was fertile, he was later told by his friend that he had fathered, in case he might wish to donate again in the future. He does not know who the mother is. Despite this experience he is dubious about donating to sperm banks. 'Because I don't know who's controlling the sperm. I do think one has the right to ask that. Once you get into a sperm bank, you get into computerland and you don't know where it's going. I'd put myself on a gynaecologist's list on the conditions I agreed to in this instance – that it's a wanted child.'

To our second question, what reaction he had to women seeking AID for reasons other than infertility, Dr James pointed out that the implications of this have yet to be fully realized. 'We are the first generation,' he said, 'where it has become possible to separate sex and reproduction. This has put us considerably off balance. We are only only just starting to work on the implications of that sociologically. Is this a good moment to start understanding a bit more about whether it's all right to have reproduction and sexuality separated? If so, how are we going to cope and what are the implications? I think there couldn't be a better time in a way. This is what you'd do in any other scientific field, if you wanted to understand a bit more. You would take a very specific example where the circumstances are as uncomplicated as you can make them. Many people, I think, accept that both men's and women's views about female sexuality are changing and even the nature of female sexuality may be changing, as it's released from reproduction.'

The implications of their actions have not, of course, escaped the women themselves. Many lesbian mothers who have chosen AID in order to conceive their children wrote to us expressing the reasons for their decision and their feelings about the implications. Betty, for example, wrote: 'I chose AID because of not wanting any future legal battles over custody at any later date. I do not want the trauma of having sexual intercourse with a man, as I could never relax enough to conceive a child. Also I believe women can live independently from men as lesbian mothers. My mother is the only person in my family who knows. She seemed very happy at the prospect of her daughter having a child, and felt AID was the best solution, as she has finally accepted after ten or eleven years that I will never resign myself to that state of legalized prostitution called marriage. And she also accepts my rights as a woman to become a mother. I shall be completely honest with the child about AID and explain the reasons why I didn't want a man in my home.' Betty's partner, Lucy, added, 'I think AID is giving lesbians who want to become mothers a real chance to be independent of men making claims on children. I hope that it will become available to any woman who feels the need to become a mother in this way.'

Elaine had her first child through a casual heterosexual encounter. Later, already settled in a lesbian partnership, she decided to use AID for her second child. She wrote that it was 'the only method acceptable to us both. I didn't want to know personally the other person involved. I feel much more secure this time and feel that I am no longer alone in a world with no future. This time I have a family and don't feel that I am a "single mum". I do sometimes feel apprehensive about what other people say or think. Not everyone in my family knows about it yet, but those who do have had a favourable reaction. There have been two incidents that I am aware of, where people have been unpleasant: a) a hostile publican, who made obscene remarks about us bringing up a child; b) a headmistress who once expressed concern to a social worker about my daughter "growing up in a lesbian household". Her teachers, though, have all been very good and pleasant to us.

'I shall always be honest with my children, right from the

start. Our love is simply a variation on a theme and is equally
as good and true as any other love. If something seems *right* to
a person then it *is* right, no matter who says otherwise. We are
just *one* part of a world which has many worlds within it. I
shall be truthful with my son when he asks. He was more
"thought out", planned and discussed beforehand than the
"average" child, and the choice to go ahead against all the social
odds makes him very much a wanted child. AID and adoption
should be more available to single women as well as gay
women.'

Liz and Anne, whose second child was conceived by AID,
had a similar response. Because AID 'didn't personally involve
a third party it seemed more practical,' wrote Anne. 'We didn't
discuss it with the family. We told a few close friends who were
interested and supportive. We did wonder what reasons the
donor had for being a donor. I'd like to think it was a desire
to help – like blood donors. Or perhaps it was a student who
would find the fee helpful. We shall tell our children that lesbianism is a valid alternative to the male-female relationship and
that we freely chose our way of living.'

When we went to visit Liz and Anne, we asked Anne more
about her experiences of AID. She told us she had had only two
inseminations and had become pregnant immediately. She inser-
ted the semen herself. Her pregnancy was perfectly normal,
except that she suffered badly with morning-sickness, as she had
with her first pregnancy. We enquired whether she had felt any
different psychological pressure or anxiety, to which she replied
that she had been more anxious with the first pregnancy. She
had not worried about using AID, once pregnant, as she and
Liz had discussed it and covered all the problems they could
think of before going ahead. We asked if it had taken a long
time to decide. They said it had, but that they decided it was
impossible for them to have another child in the same way as the
first, that is, with the help of a male friend. When we asked if
they would use AID again, if they wanted more children, they
replied that they would, but that it was not specially important
to have the same donor. Did they see any consequences for others
in their choice? 'It would be true to say we did it for ourselves,'
Liz replied, 'rather than to provide an alternative culture. We

thought a lot about how children are brought up, unlike most parents, and I feel we have got a lot to offer.' We asked if any of the doctors involved with the pregnancy had known that it was due to AID. Anne said, 'I didn't tell them, and they didn't ask. They asked me what contraception I was going to use! I remember – on the front of my notes they wrote – "Mother wants to keep baby". The DHSS officer asked me if I knew who the father was. I said "Yes", that he was a student, but that I wouldn't give his name. They asked me a few times in the first year. They are liable to do routine checks in the first year. A real nasty one came here first after James was born. I suppose they send the heavies in straight away. He said did I know who the father was? And "What about public money?" Fortunately Liz was there and battled. He was horrible. But I have since seen several very nice and helpful DHSS officers.'

Jenny and Sally, living in Australia, have two AID children. They chose this method because of the anonymity of the father and the genetic selection of the father by a third person. 'We shall explain to our children,' Sally wrote, 'that while most men love women and most women love men, some men love men and some women love women, and we are two of those women. John is now three and three-quarters and has been going to the pre-school full time for a few months. He thoroughly enjoys it and happily paints, draws, plays and sings. He *is* beautiful. Thomas is also beautiful at last, though in a more traditional way. He is even more intelligent than John and has a very irritating sense of humour, coupled with the loudest scream in the co-op. He is minded by a German woman – ferociously cross-eyed – whom he loves. He loves the other children minded there too. Actually he loves everybody, and dogs.

'Jenny thus has regained the freedom to work, which she so desperately needed, and has a good job in the public service, working a minimum of twenty-five hours a week. She is well and happy and *detests* being described as "an attractive mother of two".'

Artificial insemination by donor is practised extensively in the United Kingdom, the United States and Israel, and to a more limited extent in Australia. South Africa, France, Germany, Scandinavia, Belgium and the Netherlands. Although accurate figures are impossible to obtain, estimates suggest that millions of children have now been conceived by AID, and probably more than 100,000 in Britain alone.

AID is not against the law in Britain. The Feversham Committee, appointed in 1959 to 'enquire into the existing practice of human artificial insemination and its legal consequences', recommended in its Report that AID should constitute a 'liberty'. A liberty is defined in law as 'that sphere of activity within which the law is content to leave me alone'.

In the United States there is no Federal ruling on the subject. Each State has its own law in regard to AID; for example, in New York State only a doctor or a qualified nurse may administer it. Nevertheless, self-help groups of women and men, all over America, are using AID. There is similarly no parliamentary legislation on AID in France, Denmark or Finland.

In the former British dependencies, whose social institutions are based on British models, there are no *legal* obstacles to lesbians receiving AID, as far as we can discover. However, a doctor speaking from the Canadian High Commission in London told us that the practice, in all the Canadian provinces, was to obtain the husband's permission in cases of AID. In his own experience he had never known or heard of any lesbians requesting AID. He volunteered that his own personal view was that no doctor would administer AID to lesbian couples or to a single heterosexual woman. However, the decision ultimately rested with the doctor and the patient, since AID could only be administered by a doctor. Similarly, a spokeswoman for the Women's Advisory Bureau, employed by the Commonwealth Government of Australia, told us that she knew of no law prohibiting the use of AID for unmarried women, but that she had never heard of such a request being made and that the Australian Medical Association had issued no guidelines that she knew of on the matter. As in Canada, nevertheless, such a decision would ultimately rest with the individual doctor consulted.

We were informed by the NVSH (Dutch Society for Sexual Reform) that in Holland single women – lesbian and non-lesbian – may legally be given AID and that this practice is emotionally accepted by the public – in fact, more and more women were choosing this method. An official in the West German Federal Ministry for Family and Health explained that there is no section of criminal law specifically forbidding the use of AID for anyone, but that each case would have to be treated individually with respect to other precepts in German law, such as whether or not harmful interference with the body had occurred, whether or not such a child might have a right to know its genetic paternity, and so on. It seems fairly clear that in the absence of laws specifically concerned with AID, recourse to existing laws on related issues might be made. A reply from the Swedish Embassy stated that in Sweden the question of AID and its use is up to the doctor in each separate case. The general attitude to AID is probably hesitant; nevertheless, homosexuality *per se* is not regarded in Sweden as anything shameful.

Although AID is not against the law in most western countries, its practice has generally remained in the hands of the medical profession, and many doctors have been reluctant to recommend or administer it, even for heterosexual married couples. In the *British Journal of Sexual Medicine* for February 1977, in an article entitled 'Andrological Aspects of Sexual Medicine : Artificial Insemination by Donor', Dr G. Barry Carruthers reported on the results of a survey of 1,000 couples who were given AID between 1968 and 1973. The treatment was restricted to 'heterosexual couples with an established relationship'. Even so, 'nearly two-thirds of the group first had their attention drawn to the possibility of AID by the national media, particularly women's magazines, and less than a quarter had had their attention drawn to the possibility by their medical advisors . . . almost one in five of those who had raised the subject had been given the impression that their doctor regarded the subject as unethical or even immoral. . . .'

One result of this attitude on the part of doctors has been that the majority of people seeking AID have been middle class, highly motivated and of above average intelligence. This 'distinct upgrade in social grouping could be explained by the restricted facilities and negative professional attitude which would make it more difficult for those of the lower social categories to find their way through to treatment,' Carruthers comments. But, 'As

AID becomes more generally accepted and available it seems likely that these sociological aspects will become more averaged.'

Since AID began to be practised widely in the 1950s and '60s, there has been a continuous debate about the ethics and morality of its use. Conservative religious opinion has condemned it. Legal authorities have discussed at length its repercussions in the fields of legitimacy and inheritance. Specialists in mental health have debated its psychological and emotional consequences for the families involved. (For a full, if idiosyncratic, survey and discussion of all these points, see *Blizzard and the Holy Ghost*, by Joseph Blizzard, Peter Owen, 1977.)

Most of these people, however, approach AID entirely as a therapy for infertile men and their wives, rather than for lesbian couples or single women. Furthermore, it seems that even heterosexual couples are prepared to override previously-held principles in their desire for a child. Dr Carruthers noted, for instance, that 'couples were also prepared to act against their religious instruction where this might be antagonistic to the principle'. And Joseph Blizzard has summed up very well the feelings of an intending AID parent : 'I cannot accept dogma as the arbiter of private human conduct. . . . The participants in AID must square the process with their principles. They should think long and hard about the step they are proposing to take. They should even – if they are that sort of person – examine the views of the leaders of their religion on AID. But the final decision is theirs and theirs alone, and must be made according to their own principles.'

Blizzard, a doctor, writes illuminatingly on the psychological problems caused by infertility. However, because male infertility was the original proving-ground for the introduction of AID, it does not mean that infertility should remain the sole reason for its use.

Of the problems connected with AID and identified by the 'experts', two *are* possibly relevant to lesbian mothers and deserve consideration. The first is the possibility of future incestuous relationships, particularly when the semen of one donor is used frequently.

In fact, the chances of incest occurring are minimal. The Feversham Report stated : 'We have been informed that if 2,000

live children per year were to be born in Great Britain as a result
of the successful use of AID, and if each donor were responsible
for five children, an unwitting incestuous marriage is unlikely to
occur more than one in about fifty to a hundred years.' Furthermore, it has also been reported (by A. McLaren and A. Sparkes
in the *Journal of Biosocial Sciences*, No. 5, 1973, p. 209) that 'a
survey of blood groups of rhesus negative women in a London
suburb had revealed that no less than thirty per cent of babies
could not have been the children of the father named in the
birth register.' As the Fourth Study Group of the Royal College
of Obstetricians and Gynaecologists comment in their report
Artificial Insemination (1976): 'So not only then is the risk of
consanguineous marriage of AID offspring extremely small but
it probably also is insignificant in proportion to the problems
attributable to irregular unions, at least in London. With most
Western nations having 10 per cent of conceptions non-marital,
and with the very real possibility of marriage dying out as a
state institution, the so-called problems of incestuous relationships
can probably be forgotten. Where incest is a serious problem it
seems to be based on common upbringing rather than a common
genetic background.'

The second difficulty, and one that every AID mother has to
come to terms with, is that, strictly speaking, every AID baby
is illegitimate. Under the law, a baby conceived by AID should
be registered as 'father unknown'. That this situation is patently
ludicrous is revealed by the Feversham Committee's admission
that 'We have been told of only two occasions hitherto on which
the registrar was informed that there had been AID.' The particular consequences of this absurdity, and those of illegitimacy
generally, are examined in Chapter 6, but as AID becomes more
common and widespread, and general social attitudes change, it
is not unrealistic to expect a substantial revision of the whole
legal concept of legitimacy.

In Britain, AID is not generally available on the National
Health Service, but there are an increasing number of centres
in the country where it may be obtained, sometimes on a private
or fee-paying basis. The Royal College of Obstetricians and
Gynaecologists recommends that the initial approach should
be made through a general practitioner and then a gynaecological

(or infertility) clinic. 'In case of difficulty,' it says, 'a direct approach to the clinic will be considered sympathetically.' Single women (lesbian and non-lesbian), who may experience difficulties with their GPs, are welcome at the clinics of the British Pregnancy Advisory Service, but BPAS warns that it has long waiting lists.

The Royal College recognizes that there is a 'substantial and growing demand for AID which existing services are unable to meet in full', and it encourages the 'setting-up of new AID facilities in centres around the country, to fill the gaps in the present service. Ideally, no patient should have to travel more than 40 miles for this treatment, and waiting lists for AID treatment should be kept to a maximum of six months.'

If, as has been suggested, not all doctors are sympathetic to requests for AID from married heterosexual women, they are likely to look even less kindly at lesbians. Nevertheless there are, as we have seen, sympathetic gynaecologists who are willing to provide AID for lesbians, and a recent decision at the British Medical Association's annual conference suggests that their number is on the increase.

At the BMA's 1979 conference a proposal 'That this meeting considers that artificial insemination by a donor for lesbian couples is unethical' was lost by 162 votes to 148. Summing up, the Central Ethical Committee chairman, Dr M. J. G. Thomas, said, 'To vote against is to vote that you as individual doctors keep your right to make up your minds about an individual doctor-patient relationship. This is not a moral issue; it is the protection of your right to practise medicine as it has always been practised in this country.'

There is, furthermore, an alternative to approaching AID through the medical services. Lesbians, and other women, have the option of performing AID themselves, either independently or as part of a self-help group. AID without medical supervision is quite legal in Britain and has been practised successfully by a number of women.

Those who wish to perform AID themselves must first decide whether they intend to adopt as many as possible of the medical techniques and safeguards used by established AID clinics, or whether they merely wish to approximate to the conditions usually applying to heterosexual vaginal intercourse outside the medical context. In each case the procedure for administering AID is basically the same; the 'medical' approach, however, lays much greater emphasis on the steps to be taken *before* AID is administered, to ensure that the sperm is of the highest possible quality.

For those who are considering setting up a self-help AID group, the following guidelines may be useful. They are based on the suggestions of the AID Subcommittee of the Royal College of Obstetricians and Gynaecologists and more informal but no less pertinent advice received from 'Donna', a midwife who directs an AID service in San Francisco.

1 Selection of donors

The AID Subcommittee recommends that donors are 'best recruited by personal contact, and open advertising should be avoided. They should satisfy the following criteria :

1 Reasonable intelligence
2 No personal or family history of inheritable disorders, as obtained at interview.
3 No personal history of potentially transmissible infection (e.g. venereal disease or hepatitis)
4 An acceptable physical appearance
5 A responsible attitude
6 Good fertility, as evaluated by semen analysis

The donors should be told to report any symptoms of, or contact with, infectious diseases. They can with advantage be checked periodically by culture of semen samples for gonococci.

'Consideration should be given to limiting the number of pregnancies from any one donor (e.g. up to 20).'

2 Selection of semen

According to AID Subcommittee, 'All semen samples should be microscoped before use to ensure that they have :

1 An acceptable sperm count
2 An acceptable motility (at least 60 per cent in fresh specimens and 40 per cent in thawed frozen specimens)
3 An acceptable abnormality rate (less than 30 per cent)
4 Absence of inflammatory cells. . . .'

Donna wrote: 'I strongly recommend that a sperm count be
done of every donor prior to using him. This should include a
3-4 hour motility study done at intervals (it's no good to have a
good *count* without adequate motility over the long haul); in
reading the results of the test you should have well over 20,000,000
per millilitre. I would not use anyone under 35,000,000 if I
could possibly avoid it.

'The donor should abstain from alcohol, cigarettes and *hot*
tubs or baths for at least 72 hours (3 days) *prior* to the day the
sample is obtained for the lab test. In addition he should not
ejaculate at all for three days prior to the test in order to give
his body time to get the highest count he can. (This same procedure should be followed prior to every insemination series each
month.)

'The lab should receive the specimen in a clean *glass* jar with
a lid, kept in a brown bag (sperm are sensitive to light, heat, air),
hopefully no later than half an hour after ejaculation. A
good lab will begin the motility study upon the arrival of the
specimen. The initial motility should be no lower than 70 per
cent. In addition there should be normal viscosity and absolutely no more than 10-15 per cent abnormal sperm (that is
the morphology number given). The closer the actual sperm
count is to 50,000,000 or better, the better it is for your
chances.

'*Very important* – if there is a white blood cell count, find
out if it's considered high: it can show evidence of infection
present in the donor. *Don't use him* until it's checked out OK
by a doctor or a lab. Which brings me to VD: each and every
donor should be given the facts regarding what those diseases
do to offspring and mothers *as well as* themselves. All donors
(unless you are absolutely convinced they are celibate or monogamous *and* have been tested clean once for both syphilis and GC
as well as *herpes*) should be tested well enough in advance of each

month's ovulatory period that any positive results can be gotten *prior* to the time you need to use his sperm.

'Lastly some things I've noticed in getting donors screened for fertility – those with the *lowest* overall fertility are heavy red meat eaters, take no vitamins, drink copiously or smoke more than a packet of cigarettes a day. Also you should be aware that many prescription drugs adversely affect *not just* sperm counts and *apparent* fertility (through lab tests – semen analysis), but can actually alter the DNA makeup without visibly altering the semen analysis. For a thoroughly scary, but vitally important, bit of information on all of this, order a copy of *Co Evolution Quarterly* number 21. Spring 1979's whole issue was on Genetic Toxicity – and vital reading for anyone intending to get pregnant these days. (*Co Evolution Quarterly* is available from PO Box 428, Sausalito, California 94965, USA.) The P.D.R. (*Physician's Desk Reference*) lists drugs which should be avoided by women 'of child-bearing age', but has never listed stuff men of child-bearing age should avoid. Similar hazards affect men's fertility in the same or related ways.'

3 Counselling

AID is still new and no intending mother will consider it without wanting to discuss the implications. The counsellor should be a sympathetic person who knows something about the intending mother and about children, or, even better, an AID mother. The discussion should involve both partners from the start.

4 Sex predetermination

'Of the lesbian mothers (through AID) I know in the Bay area (San Francisco region),' wrote Donna, 'nearly all of whom definitely preferred rearing a female child, approximately 93 per cent bore male children. This is despite the fact that most followed the sex predetermination techniques set forth by Tandrum Shettles (the acid/alkaline douching and timing of insemination relating to ovulation, etc.). It seems that well over 80 per cent of women who are artificially inseminated bear male children. No one is very clear why.

'To better research the various sex selection techniques around I scouted out an article by Robert H. Glass M.M., F.A.C.O.G. called "Sex Preselection" which was published in *Obstetrics – Gynaecology*, Vol. 49, No. 1, January 1977, by the Medical Department of Harper & Row Publishers Inc. The basic information is that there are no scientifically documented methods of sex preselection which actually work, with the possible exception of one which involves *immobilized* sperm – later changed in further experiments to live or motile sperm – layered with liquid bovine serum albumin. I won't recount all of this experiment – suffice it to say it's not an easy, accessible method, has "promise", but hasn't actually been *disproved* as are, so far, all other methods which have been suggested.

'This article deals with all methods that had been suggested up to that time, and when I recently talked with Dr Glass I found nothing new to add to his findings. I am confident that if something of promise had been developed he would have heard of it. For reprints of his article write to : Robert Glass M.D., Dept of Obstetrics and Gynaecology, School of Medicine, University of California, San Francisco, California 94143, USA.'

The scientific nature of some of these techniques may seem over-elaborate to intending mothers. They have been devised by doctors partly for their own protection and partly as a means to further scientific knowledge. 'Natural' insemination, after all, is not characterized by any of these procedures – a wife rarely enquires about her husband's sperm count, motility or genetic toxicity. And the 'artificiality' of AID simply involves the substitution of a syringe for a penis.

For those who are concerned only to find an alternative to heterosexual vaginal intercourse as a means of conceiving a child, the basic procedure for AID is as follows :

1. Be able to predict when you will ovulate. Do this by preparing a temperature chart. Take a piece of graph paper; along the bottom axis, mark off successive points and number them, one for each day of the month. Along the side axis, mark off points for your temperature, from one degree below normal to

two degrees above normal and allowing enough space to calculate within tenths of a degree. Each morning, as soon as you awake, take your temperature. You must leave the thermometer in your mouth for at least two minutes and you must take your temperature before doing *anything* else – before drinking tea, smoking, going to the lavatory, getting out of bed, etc. When you are ovulating, your temperature will rise, but only by a small amount, tenths of a degree even. So to get accurate readings, you must do it at the same time – in the morning – and before any activity, because activity *of any sort* will also raise your body temperature by tenths of a degree. Most women ovulate on the twelfth to fourteenth day after their last period, but each woman is different and you can only be really sure about your own fertile span by preparing a chart.

2. After taking your chart for three months, you will have a pretty good idea when your next ovulation is due. By now, you should have selected a donor or asked the help of a friend to select a donor. Selection of a donor should be based on physical fitness, freedom from disease, a good family history and intelligence.

3. When you are fertile, arrange for the donor to ejaculate into a *clean* container. The container should be of a suitable size to allow a syringe to draw up the semen. Use the semen, if possible, within two hours. It will last longer, but after two hours the sperm begin to die in large numbers.

4. Use a *clean* syringe, without a needle, to draw up the semen from the container. Insert the syringe into the vagina just as you insert a tampon. Press the plunger. It is *not* necessary to dilate the cervix. Then lie with your bottom raised on some cushions for about twenty minutes, so that the semen does not have a chance to leak out.

(Donna, the midwife who wrote to us from San Francisco, recommends using a diaphragm, 'since it keeps the sperm close to where it needs to be, and not dripping out of you. . . . It should be a new diaphragm fitted specifically for the woman who will use it. Try it out *prior to* the day you need to use it. Birth control fitters of diaphragms sometimes give a size slightly too large and if it's so uncomfortable you can't leave it inside for 24 hours without cramping, you need a smaller size.

'I recommend using a plastic 3cc syringe *without* needle to introduce the ejaculate into the diaphragm (or vagina – the diaphragm isn't absolutely necessary; it just ups the odds). The syringe is safe, about the right size, non-irritating. An eye-dropper tends to keep some sperm in it and is harder to use. Generally you need only one or two syringes' full to introduce an entire ejaculate, versus four to five eye dropper loads – the risk being that the eye dropper will cause leakage from continual irritation of the outer vaginal muscles which can contract and force sperm out.')

5. It is up to you how many inseminations you do. One woman, to make quite sure she became pregnant, had an insemination every day for five days, starting on the first day of her ovulation. Doctors and clinics tend to do only one or two inseminations per cycle but there is no reason why you should follow this clinical practice. If you wanted to become pregnant from sexual intercourse, after all, you would simply have sex with your partner as often as possible during your fertile span.

6. If you do not become pregnant during the first cycle, repeat the same procedure the following month. If you do not become pregnant over a longer period, you must change the donor. If you still fail to become pregnant, you must go through some medical investigation of your own fertility.

7. A donor is entitled to legitimate compensation for any expenses he has incurred. But he ought not to be paid for his semen. This is a quick and simple way of eliminating disreputable characters who may not tell the truth about their physical condition. If there is no financial reward, their motivation is likely to be humane and sympathetic.

8. If you use AID, you are not obliged to tell *anyone* that you have done so. Equally, if you do wish to tell anyone, you are free to do so. You have not done anything illegal.

If you wish to discuss the implications of AID before embarking on it – and most women do – choose a sympathetic friend or counsellor, or, better still, an AID mother, with whom to discuss your particular queries. If you do not know such a person, one of the lesbian organizations, such as Sappho, will help you.

Once you are pregnant, make your plans in the same way as other expectant mothers do. Register for ante-natal care, choose which method of birth you want and prepare for it. If you do not wish to tell the social and medical personnel that your baby is the result of AID, simply say that the father is unknown. That, anyway, is the truth.

5 Children and Families

We have already noted that a recent investigation found no differences between children brought up by lesbians and children brought up by heterosexual single parents. In this chapter we look at what some children have to say about what it is like to live with a lesbian mother (with or without lesbian lovers). We also explore in some detail the effects of a mother's lesbianism on her family, including her husband.

The children we talked to ranged between eight and twenty-one years of age. Among the youngest were Sylvia's two daughters, Simone, aged eleven, and Nancy, aged eight. We spoke to them together.

Simone said that her mother's lesbianism had aroused no unpleasantness at school, and that when she takes friends home she introduces her mother's lover by saying, 'This is Kirstin and she's living with my mum.' After talking for a while, the discussion moved on to 'love'. Nancy asked, 'What kind of love are we talking about? Say there was a teenager in love with a teenager and one was a boy and one was a girl, and they loved each other. That's what I'd take it as. And like Mummy and Kirstin.' What about herself and Mummy? we asked. 'I love her and she loves me. That's love,' Nancy replied.

Sylvia told us, 'Nancy was sitting in the bath the other night and gave me a nice little homily about how she needn't worry too much about me now, when she's living with Daddy, because I'd now got another daddy, Kirstin, who could look after me. I sort of fell about and said, "No, no, no." ' Nancy then tried to explain what she had meant. 'But she is like – well, say she's not a man, but she's still like a husband. She keeps you company, like most husbands. I don't know why people do get married. . . . What do they do when they're married. . . ? Just live together. . . ?' Simone answered her, 'So if they have a child, then it isn't a bastard.' Nancy then told us, 'The only reason I love Kirstin is that she's keeping Mummy from crying, when we go to Daddy. She'll keep Mummy okay.'

Simone told us she didn't want to get married and have children, but Nancy said, 'I haven't thought about it properly, because I'm only going to think about that when I'm old enough. 'Cos when you're seven, you say, "I'm going to do that." And then I'm not going to do what I said when I was seven!'

Penny's daughter, Jean, aged twelve, said she doesn't tell her friends her mother is gay, nor does she keep it a secret. She takes her friends home and they sometimes ask where her dad is. 'That's a good question!' she said. 'I wouldn't really want one. My friends say, "I can't be late – my dad might hit me." You don't have those fears from your mum. She says, "Get in by ten", but she wouldn't hit me. Most men come in drunk all the time. Mum doesn't do that sort of thing. My mum is better than most mums I know. Some mums have a dad and ask dad to wallop the kids.' Jean told us she wanted to grow up, get married, 'have two children and then get divorced quickly'. She said she had kissed both boys and girls and that it all felt quite natural. We asked her why she would want to get divorced. 'He might get on my nerves,' she said. 'If he doesn't take his turn at doing the washing-up, then I will divorce him.' Finally she wanted to say, 'We're happy with our mum as she is and it hasn't disturbed either of us – me or my brother.'

Tom, aged thirteen, lives with his mother, Pat, his mother's lover, Sal, and his three-year-old brother, Terry. 'I just mix with people who can understand,' Tom said. 'Those who mock me or laugh at me – I don't talk to them. The only people I let know are my friends who don't mind. Most of them are quite interested.'

How do the others mock? 'Oh,' he said, 'as mum's gay, I've got to be gay as well, being in a gay home. It doesn't make any difference to me, whether I am or not.'

How did they know his mum is gay? 'A long time ago,' he said, 'I used to have a really big mouth and it got me into a lot of name-calling. I was about seven or eight. It upset me. But since then I've learned – why bother to tell? No one's really against gays where I go and play.'

We asked what sort of interest his friends showed. 'They'd say, "I've never met a gay family before. Can I come and meet your parents?" Normally we go and sit in my room. They say that their best friends are with people who are gay.'

Then we asked Tom how much he minded not having a dad. He said he didn't mind, 'because most of the blokes have divorced fathers. I prefer to have two sorts of mothers.'

Did he want to be a father himself? 'I'd quite like to be a dad,' he said. 'To see what I'm like with children. To see if I could bring them up well.' What did he mean? 'Obviously there's got to be certain rules,' he replied, 'such as not spoiling them rotten. They would do what they're told. On the other hand, if it wasn't too expensive, I'd give them a treat every so often. I'd play with them every day when I came home from work. I'd have a boy and a girl.' Would he treat them differently? we asked. 'When the girl was about thirteen, I wouldn't let her out late – just the normal precautions, you know.' What were the normal precautions? 'Well, going out late at night with anybody.' We asked whether boys didn't need that kind of protection. 'Well, very little,' he said. 'Paedophilia is one aspect. It's more likely to happen to a girl than a boy. Also you never know what sort of boy your daughter's going out with – you've got to keep a good eye on that.'

We wondered if his mother had told him about sex. 'Oh yes. Ages ago. I have a record of how I was born, which I listened to. I asked her questions and she told me.' Had he been pleased when his brother Terry was born? 'I remember when he was born,' Tom said. 'I got news of it just after I'd been playing in a Cub Scouts football match. I was so thrilled. I wasn't bothered at all that my mum had – obviously – gone to bed with a guy to get Terry. The fact was, I had a brother, which I'd always wanted from the age of about seven. I wouldn't really want her to have another baby now. She hasn't really got that much money to keep three kids.'

After that, he wanted to add, 'I think we should say there's no differences between homosexuals and heterosexuals to the child. Why shouldn't two women or two guys bring up a child? If you want a child and can look after it, it doesn't matter what home it's brought up in.'

We asked if he had ever been physically attacked on account of his mother's lesbianism. 'I and a friend, we didn't like each other much,' he said. 'Walking home, he started calling my mum names: "queer", "lezzie". I got pretty upset about that. He was mocking me, so I mocked him. Then he slapped me. I walked on, following him. He stopped, turned round. I hit him square on the jaw. He ran home crying. I walked home feeling very unhappy. He didn't do it again. That was the only time it happened.'

Should lesbians be able to have children? we asked. 'They're people too. Why shouldn't they?' he replied.

Penny's son, Michael, aged sixteen, said his friends assumed his mother was divorced and it wouldn't occur to them to ask if she were gay. Was he afraid of people in general knowing that she was gay? 'Obviously not,' he said. 'She's got *a lot* of friends. They're unusual. I was reading this book *We're Here* and they said, "We're out of our closets!" And I thought of all Penny's friends and I said, "They should get back in." And now it's become a joke – "Shove 'em back in!" It struck me as funny.'

We asked him if he could remember his father. Michael said he was three or four when his father left and that he could remember him clearly. 'If he opened the beer, I thought, "Oh-oh, Daddy's going to change again," you know – and I used to hide his beer and things like that.' Why did he hide the beer? 'He turned aggressive – under alcohol – on my mum. He resented my mum and me,' he said. 'I suppose it was something to do with me – that she gave me affection.' Did he feel he had missed out, growing up in a home without a dad? 'No,' he said, 'I've seen quite a lot of them [dads].'

He explained that when he visited his friends' houses during times when the father was at home, he couldn't relax. 'Well – the dad runs it,' he explained, 'because he comes straight in and "Hello, love" – and the wife's making tea. They're [the fathers] very strict – and I make conversation but it's not the same as with the mums. The dads, see, they come home from work and they're in a foul mood – and straight up into a scene and things like that.'

We asked if he thought his mother had done him any harm

by being gay. 'No, no way,' he said. 'All the lesbians I've known, they've loved their kids of any sex. All the ones who've wanted kids, couldn't have cared less about wanting a boy or a girl.'

What about his own sexual interest? 'When I was about eight or nine or something,' he began, 'there was this girl named Zoe – she was fourteen actually – and I "come off" sex with Zoe. Masturbation come after sex with Zoe. I used to masturbate, but not thinking of sex, and then when I met Zoe, I had sex and that was all right. I remember in the next couple of days I masturbated thinking of sex. I learned contraception from men. And the responsibility.' We asked whether, with Zoe, he had connected sex with pregnancy. He said he had not. 'A couple of months later,' he went on, 'when we played mummies and daddies, me and Zoe (you see, we used to play mummies and daddies quite a lot), I asked her how you had a baby. She told me it was by what we did. I asked her if she was going to have a baby. She said no. She just said we were too young.'

Michael went on to say that he thought the sort of family life he'd had had made him more broadminded. Once a girl had talked to him about fancying another girl, and he'd said to her, 'Go ahead and enjoy it.' He seemed to get a 'rush' of friends wanting to talk about themselves and about sex; he thought this was 'probably because they knew I was the last one to shout about it.' He wants to be a father himself, but not while he is so young.

Finally, we talked at some length to all the members of one family. The mother, Jane, is a professional woman now living alone in a new house, planned by herself and her lesbian lover, in the East Midlands. Edwin, a company executive, lives with their son Miles, an eighteen-year-old student, Miles' girl-friend Gerry, and Rae, Jane and Edwin's thirteen-year-old daughter, in a separate house not far away. Sue, the eldest daughter, is a nineteen-year-old secretary; she shares a flat with her lesbian lover. Jane's lover, Miriam, lives in a flat nearby and works in a travel agency.

The experiences of Jane and Edwin, and of the family generally, show the possibilities of an anti-patriarchal friendship between a lesbian mother and the father of her children. Although separated, Jane and Edwin obviously feel the warmest regard for one another, and Edwin, in particular, is devoted to his three children. They, in their turn, clearly have very few secrets from either of their parents.

Jane and Edwin met when they were very young. 'I was in the services from the time I left University,' Edwin explained, 'but we'd known each other since she was fifteen and I was seventeen. It was a childhood romance on my part. The experience of the other had been the only real experience that we had of sexuality – love – call it what you will.' Jane went on, 'Marriage was something I never sought positively. It was an inevitable end result to the friendship that we had and the power of the love he had for me. I rather allowed myself to be taken in to marriage, because I was an easy-going person. Hindsight says that marriage was never, ever, something I wanted positively, for myself.'

The pressure of marriage disturbed their relationship traumatically. Jane explained : 'When we were courting, Edwin was a sexual young man, just as I was a sexual young woman. I found him very beautiful, extremely physically beautiful. His need for sex stopped as soon as we married. It changed with him. It disappeared. I was driven insane by my sexual needs which were not satisfied. After eighteen months we went to the Marriage Guidance Council. The Guidance Counsellor established that Edwin was suffering from the madonna/whore syndrome. This stemmed from his early upbringing that women are to be respected and whores are to be made love to, but you don't combine the two.' They worked at their relationship, however, and had their three children.

Rae, with the wisdom of innocence, put into a nutshell the role-reversal which characterizes the friendship between her parents : 'My father was a perfect mother. My mother was a perfect father.' Edwin explained, 'I've always adored the thought of being a father, from the earliest age I can remember. Being a father is providing a material background, but particularly friendship and support for people who are growing and maturing, to enable them to achieve their full potential. I helped with everything. I was better at changing nappies than Jane. I was better at bathing. I was better at feeding and I was better at burping them. I didn't see how I could be supportive without doing the practical things as well. I've always felt towards my children as I understand most mothers feel towards their children.' Jane had the same perception. 'I work in the maternity wards,' she said, 'and my job is to teach ante-natal patients parenthood. The example I have used for the last five years is Edwin, as to how it should be done. I also teach young fathers, using Edwin as the prime example of good motherhood and fatherhood.' What children need, they seemed to be agreeing, is good mothering – care, love and nurture – and that good mothering can be done either by a woman or by a man. The patriarchal concept of fathering – the exerting of power, discipline and authority – was not in evidence in this family.

After the birth of their third child, Jane fell in love with another woman. Edwin's friendship for Jane remained firm. 'I am a lesbian,' Jane said. 'I knew I was when I was about thirty. Just after I'd given birth to Rae, I fell hopelessly in love with one of the other officer's wives in Singapore. The feelings I felt for her were in excess of anything I'd felt before. It was the sort of thing one heard about and had seen on films, but thought, "This isn't true." It was romantic passion. When I felt this for another woman, I realized, to my horror, this was homosexuality. The fact that I had a husband and three children made it difficult to accommodate. I told my husband about it. As always, he was totally gentle, kind and equally thrown, but he didn't show it. Together we tried to live through it – get over it. We were both very naïve, very well brought up, and knew nothing about homosexuality. We were in the kitchen and I said, "I have fallen in love with Vicki." He said nothing. He put his arms around me and I put mine around him and we held each other very, very tight. I don't think we said anything else.'

Edwin broke in, 'I remember I said, "I can quite understand it. Most people seem to." I was in love with Vicki, but not in the same sense as Jane. Vicki was that sort of person. She was a magic sort of person.' We asked Edwin how he had felt about Jane at that point. 'Sad,' he replied. 'I wanted to be supportive. I didn't feel sorry for her. I felt sorry for her pain. I hoped she wouldn't suffer by herself. I felt it was something we were both involved in. I hoped I'd help her get over it.'

Much later, Jane fell in love again, this time with a younger woman called Miriam. Jane and Miriam had a lesbian relationship for over seven years, while the children were growing up. Again, Edwin showed friendship and concern. 'Miriam was in a dependency situation as far as I was concerned,' he said, 'because I'd given her help with her education. She was more of a daughter to me. When the thing became permanent, I felt I'd better do the best I could. Territorial integrity has never worried me – space wasn't a worry – I've always been absolutely convinced of who I am and what I am. It doesn't bother me when people are close because I have an inner value.'

Jane's lover, Miriam, then gave her view : 'When I first moved in, it wasn't to be permanent. I'd got a job in the area and a promise of accommodation – but there was a hitch in the taking over of the accommodation for two or three weeks. Jane suggested coming and staying for that time. Then it developed from there. I've known the children since very young – over eight years. I've always got on with all three children. I love them like brothers and sisters. In fact I get on better with them than my own brothers and sisters. I met the whole family when I was sixteen. The love relationship didn't start until I was seventeen and a half. I was twenty-one when I stayed with them. I'd always been around. So long as I was near Jane, space didn't matter. As long as she was there, I didn't care where I was. I loved Edwin in the way I would have expected to love a father, had I known mine. Edwin was always helpful, kind and fatherly. I felt easy with him in a daughterly way. I never felt jealous towards any of the children at all. I occasionally felt jealous of Edwin – I wasn't there often enough for it to bother me, because when I was there, Jane's attention was almost exclusively for me.'

We asked where they had all slept, when Miriam moved in. 'They slept together,' said Edwin. 'I slept on my own.' Edwin went on to explain that he was perfectly free to find another sexual partner, whom Jane would make welcome in their house, but that he had not felt inclined to do so and that he could accept the situation as it was without difficulty.

The basic relationship demonstrated by Jane and Edwin

is a co-operative and generous friendship, which enabled Edwin to mother his children – to their evident advantage – and which helped Jane to discover and work out her lesbian sexuality. Each partner could respect the other – and each partner showed no need to reject the company and friendship of the other. It is the patriarch, the authoritarian male, the boss, who has no place in a lesbian world. People like Edwin, on the other hand, have an obvious place, and are welcome.

When we talked to the children, they all agreed that everyone had been happier since Jane and Edwin's separation; they were specially concerned about the happiness of their parents. Rae, aged thirteen, told us, 'When Mum shouted at Dad, I used to cry for him. I couldn't understand why he wouldn't cry. Everybody else cries, why couldn't he? So I used to go upstairs and cry for him. I told him once.'

When Miriam moved in to live with Jane, Rae regarded her as 'an extra hand to the housework'. 'I was five,' she said. 'I remember her coming weekends, and for holidays. I thought of her as a big sister who came to stay with us. Then she came to live with us and she became a permanent big sister. I was fed up with Sue and my brother – he was lazy, so the housework always got left to me. It always seemed to be my turn.'

We asked when she realized Miriam wasn't just a big sister. 'When Mum moved out to live with Miriam,' she said. 'Mum was arguing with Dad more often. Things were going wrong. Mum had a go at Dad, Miles and Sue, and then she had a go at me. I was crying everywhere. It was as though it was all bottled up inside her. I didn't do this. I didn't do that. Every little thing was brought out in the open. My room was untidy, or, I should wash in the morning. I didn't begin to resent Miriam until she moved out and took my mum. Then Mum and Dad told me the facts. After the talk I didn't resent Miriam. I thought originally she'd taken Mummy away. Thus she was causing a great pain for everybody. Then I found out that she had helped us all. She'd helped us all to decide what to do. Mum moved out with Miriam. Then Sue moved out to Maxine. Dad, Miles and I moved to a smaller house. Everything was perfect. We were still a family, but living in three different houses.'

During the time Miriam was living with them, Rae's protective feelings towards her father were very strong. 'Dad was sleeping on the settee,' she explained. 'Mum and Miriam were upstairs. At first I thought, "This is all right, Miriam's a guest." Dad naturally would give up his bed to her. At first I was going to, but Dad's so much of a gentleman. Then after about two weeks, I thought, "This is a bit long." I kept saying, "Isn't the settee a bit uncomfortable?" – because it's curved – "Do you mind?" I was always worrying. I kept saying, "You can have my bed, I'm smaller than you." He always replied, "I'm perfectly comfortable." It just got me, then we moved and we all had beds.'

We asked Rae if anyone at school had been nasty about her mother. 'I used to have friends coming round,' she said, 'and my parents said, "If anyone asks where your mother is, say she's on holiday or she's staying with somebody." Eventually my friends would put two and two together. Only one girl said anything that really hurt me. We were having an argument and she said, "Well, at least my mum doesn't go prancing around with girls like your mum – or like your sister." She needn't have said it like that. It was in front of so many people in my class. I couldn't answer. I was too shocked. And she's been round my home and had a good time. Whenever they've seen my mum, they say, "Isn't your mum smashing?" I couldn't understand how one day she would say my mother was smashing and the next day be horrible about her. I can't give a damn what they say. It's got nothing to do with them. I love my mum and my dad very much indeed – ever so much.'

Next we spoke to Miles, aged eighteen. He told us that he had a sexual relationship with his girl-friend which they hoped would end in marriage one day. 'But I'm not going to rush off and get married at once,' he said. 'I would like to be able to support her as well as I think she deserves to be supported. It could mean that we'd split up in fifteen to twenty years if we got married now, because we haven't developed our personalities to the full. If they develop when we're married and we develop apart, it would be a great mistake to get married at this age. She wants to hold it off, but she also wants to get married now, to have the status of housewife. That's her ambition, and to have children.'

What were his feelings towards his mother? 'I detested her until a year and a half ago, when she moved out,' he replied. 'When I found out she was gay, it didn't help me to understand her any more. And it didn't make me feel any better about the mistreatment I had from her. Apart from being a son she didn't want, which I always knew, I was also a man. I believed she had as little regard for me as I had for her. I always felt I was the one who was picked on, especially when Rae could do no wrong.' We asked if he understood what being gay meant. 'Oh yes,' he said, 'I heard it at boarding school, where you tend to learn most of the sly names for anything sexual. Gay meant homosexual – including women.

'I can't remember my mother. The only nice thing I remember about her was when I got hit by a taxi at the age of four. She brought me a panda mask in hospital, which I'd always wanted. It's the earliest nice thing I remember.'

Did he feel bitter? 'No, I'm grateful, actually,' he said. 'I think I'm a far better person than I would have been if I got the love I wanted. My girl-friend does things for me, without my asking. She gets up and makes tea in the morning. Runs the bath. Washes up. I often help with the wiping up. Occasionally she galvanizes me out of bed to make the tea.'

At this point Jane interrupted her son. 'I'm bursting to say something,' she said. 'Miles has felt always that he was unloved. The moment I had Miles – even at eighteen months – I recognized I had given birth to the gentlest of men. He is by nature a most affectionate, gentle, tender young man. I knew that we live in a rough, tough and cruel world. If I allowed this gentleness to flourish as it was, he would be destroyed. I was quite harsh, tough and hard with him, hoping it would grow old-fashioned backbone, to help support that instinctive gentleness which he had inherited from his father. The love he got from me was a tough kind. I don't love in a gentle, tender, affectionate, feminine role-playing way. The love I gave him was a father's love. Here is my son – my son must survive and the love I gave him was a masculine role-playing kind.'

Miles added, 'I don't hold any grudge, now, against my mother. I can work it out logically. She did the right thing. I've been big, butch and beefy enough to stop people pushing me around. I present an image just tough enough to keep out of trouble, but not tough enough to cause trouble.'

We asked how it had affected him that his mother was a lesbian. 'I don't think it has affected me at all,' he said. 'I think there is nothing wrong with a lesbian mother if you want to be a mother. Those who say that lesbians shouldn't have children because they may be boys are mindless idiots. They should not say that sort of thing unless they've experienced it and know that that is fact, or talk to those who have been in the situation.'

Had he thought of having children himself? 'Not seriously, no,' he said. 'Gerry and I would like to have children, if we get married, in about five or six years hence. Until then we have decided to use contraceptives in one form or another. It's for the sake of the child. I wouldn't like to have a child born out of wedlock, because I wouldn't like to put a child in a situation where it has to say, "My parents weren't married." If we had a child, then found we didn't want to live together and split up – that child would be a one-parent child who's also illegitimate. One or the other it could cope with, with love, but not both.

'I want to be a father so that I can then see myself and the person I was in love with at the time – or even still am – growing up through the years and that is a part of us. I don't believe in the family concept of a father and a mother, for a start. I believe in the concept of two parents. I don't see why they should be different sexes. I think it's totally irrelevant what sex they are, as long as they can provide for the needs of their children – material needs, love, discipline. If Gerry had a good job and the prospects were better than mine, then I think I would be prepared to stay home and be the mother. I think I would go against the cultural conditioning of "The Father".'

Sue, aged nineteen, has a lesbian lover with whom she lives. When we asked her about her feelings towards her mother, she said: 'I'd known for a long time that Mum was gay without actually being able to formulate it into a thought which I could read. I knew something wasn't right from about the age of eight. When I found out, it was like a light bulb exploding in my head and I suddenly knew why she'd behaved the way she had. From that moment onwards, I no longer felt any resentment towards her, no bitterness. I felt on a par. I was twelve or

thirteen. It made the world of difference to me. While there are
lots of things I don't know about Mum or Dad, because everybody's entitled to their own personal secrets, it was as though
there had been something gnawing away there which was upsetting me. I didn't understand exactly what it involved. A lot of
Mum's friends were gay. She was quite open about it; she'd
introduce them: "This is Alice and Emmy and they are gay".'

Sue explained that she got on much better with Jane after
being told that she was gay. 'Before that I sensed Mum was trying so hard to reach me,' she said, 'but because I had built up
such barriers, it was impossible. She was trying to give love to
me but I couldn't receive it. From the word go I've always been
a rather hysterical sort of person – up one minute, down the
next – out on the roof – "I'm going to jump off !" – "Well, you
jump off then." So I'd make to run up and she said, "No, stop." So
she had to pick the right moment before telling me. Even though
we were worlds apart, there was always a bond between us, in a
strange sort of way. I was very close to her. I had a sense she
was always trying to get through to me. That was a confidence,
something special between us. For the first time in my life she
was a human being to me.'

We asked Sue how she had entered her present relationship.
She replied, 'I went out for an evening, trying to get over my
boy-friend. I loved him. I was close to him. Basically because
when he took me out we did things. We stripped down a couple
of car engines together. He took me fishing. He took me to football matches. We never went to the movies, or held hands, or
went for walks together. He wasn't a very stimulating person to
talk to. I enjoyed his company – he had a lot of hobbies, which
I enjoyed. Apart from the feeling of warmth and having somebody close to me, I had no physical pleasure from him, or from
any of the men I went out with. I found it intensely boring for
a start. I can appreciate that a nice tanned body with muscular
shoulders, hairy chest and all that sort of thing, is attractive to
the eye. But when you get to the naughty bits, it's just a non-
event.

'I knew what happened physically in the most common posi-
tions from magazines and things we'd read. I remember Dad
saying, "A gentleman always rests on his elbows." I remember

Mum reading an article to me about ladies who wanted to get up and do something about sex, but their husbands preferred them to lie back and think of Britain! Obviously, from the way Mum was reading it, she didn't think that women should lie back and think of Britain. I picked that up. I don't think it would have made very much difference the first time, because I got no pleasure, physically, for myself, from men. I thought there must be a bit more to it than this. Just thinking about how I could make myself into a good lover. I did, in fact.'

We asked if she had masturbated and she said she had. We then asked also how her relationship with her woman lover was different. 'It had never occurred to me that I might be gay,' she said. 'In fact, because Mum was, I didn't really want to be. No way did I want to be a carbon copy of Mum. People said we were so alike in many ways, even though I looked like Dad. I walked into a night club and saw a friend I'd known at school. She said, "Hello" and stopped. We looked at each other. We've been together ever since. She's known since the age of five that she fancied girls.'

Sue said that she enjoyed the company of men but expressed relief that she no longer had any 'physical hassle'. 'I don't have to worry if my buttons are all done up,' she explained.

We asked her to tell us about her present relationship. 'We've been together eighteen months, nearly two years,' she replied. 'It's very good. There are a lot of things in a relationship that you don't admit for a very, very long time – like picking your nose. There are things in a relationship between a man and a woman, such as wives don't come to orgasm with their husbands. It's the same with boy-friends. Some things are never admitted. The mere fact that they are of different sexes means that there is something pushing them apart which makes them opposites. I think men are attracted to women because they are opposite. Men and women, in my experience, don't play together. They do things together; they go out and have a good time. Now Maxine will come and tickle me and we romp around on the floor. If we stay together till forty, we will still play. There are terms of endearment which were embarrassing at first, but now, anything that pops into my head I can say to her. I have no inhibitions about what I say or what I do.'

Did she want to be a mother? 'I have maternal instincts,' she said. 'I have a need to discipline and bring up a small creature and to make sure that it is as well adjusted as it could possibly be. To make sure they feel contented and want to come home. Maxine said she would like children, but *she'd* like to give *me* children. I wouldn't use AID because I wouldn't have a child unless it came from both our ovaries, and that isn't possible. We might adopt, but I wouldn't have a child until I'd mellowed sufficiently to give it the upbringing which I didn't have in certain areas. I wouldn't go looking for a man to have one. Because I love Maxine I feel obliged not to go with a man.

'I don't feel adversely affected that Mum and Dad have split up, or that Mum is gay and living with Miriam. I've gained from all that by being in a position to understand feelings and emotions from my straight father, sister and brother and their reactions to me. I'm open to more things because of my set-up and Mum's set-up. Through having had a lot of experiences crammed into the short time of my life, I'm more able to give comfort, understanding and help to many more people.'

These are some of the views expressed to us by lesbian families. As far as the children were concerned, they all spoke freely in front of their mothers and their mothers' lovers. The mothering styles in each family were different, but the children shared an open attitude towards sexuality, love and parenting which we found convincing and encouraging. Some of the children differentiated between men and fathers; they liked the former and not the latter.

We are not trained in any particular psychological science and we have made no pretence that ours is a 'scientific' study, but we should like to record that we saw no signs of any serious trauma in these children. As Tom's mother put it to us, 'The only way is for kids of Tom's age and upwards to say, "Here we are." I've always said : "Let's put these children in a room, work out a questionnaire, add a dozen children from heterosexual families from a comparable age. Muddle them up together. Give them the questionnaire – and you tell us which is which." I think this is the only way to do it. We'd either win or lose. We would have to stick by the decision, if the majority of children brought up by lesbians were peculiar and socially unacceptable. When Tom turns to me and says, "Why am I here?" I say, "Because I wanted you." '

6 **Ways Forward**

We are nearing the end of the century. Masters and Johnson have published the results of more than twenty years of the scientific study of human sexuality and they have found, by systematic observation, that homosexual people display no differences of physiology when compared with heterosexual people. Are there, then, any medical or psychological reasons why lesbians should not be mothers? In the expert opinion of many researchers, there are no such reasons. Much of the research, to date, has been done in the United States, where National Gay Task Force (NGTF) estimates that between 1,430,000 and 2,200,000 lesbians are mothers. NGTF have collated the results of this research and we begin this chapter by looking at some of the researchers' conclusions.

Professor Robert Gould, clinical psychiatrist at the New York Medical College, writes, 'Recent studies have shown that children raised by a homosexual parent are as sexually and emotionally well-adjusted as children raised by a heterosexual parent.' Similarly, Evelyn Hooker, a clinical psychologist from the Neuropsychiatric Institute of the University of California, notes, 'A large number of research studies have clearly demonstrated that sexual orientation in and of itself indicates nothing about attributes of personality or character, such as integrity, reliability, responsibility, or devotion to, and the ability to care for, children. Two research studies (Green and Kirkpatrick) have demonstrated that children in the custody of their lesbian mothers, when compared with children in the custody of a divorced heterosexual mother, show no differences in the degree of psychologically healthy functioning and development.' And Betty Kalis, Clinical Professor of Medical Psychology at the University of California, states, 'There is, to my knowledge, no evidence that sexual orientation or sexual preference, as such, is in any way predictive of an individual's parenting ability.'

Pepper Schwartz, a sociologist at the University of Washington, writes, 'I see no evidence of differences between homosexual and heterosexual parents. There seems to be no greater trauma for the children of gay parents, nor do these children feel unduly stigmatized or unworthy. Further, the Lesbians and homosexuals I have interviewed or interacted with are functioning in society; there does not seem to be evidence of traits that might indicate unsuitability for parenthood. Indeed, I might argue the opposite. We have noticed that in a Lesbian relationship both women tend to take a more equal interest in the children than in other "reconstituted" families. If, as has been hypothesized, children do best under conditions of attention, warmth and support from a number of adults, then Lesbian parents might be considered superior care givers and parental figures.'

Judd Marmor, Professor of Psychiatry at the University of Southern California School of Medicine, suggests that 'the problem is not with the relationship between predominantly homosexual parents and their children, but with a society which has misunderstood and denied human sexuality and most particularly that of persons whose orientation differs from the majority's. I know of no scientific evidence that the children of predominantly homosexual parents are any more or less likely to become homosexually oriented than those of heterosexuals, just as I know of no evidence that predominantly heterosexual parents are more loving, supportive, or stable in their parental roles than homosexual women and men.'

On a different theme, Clara Riley, a practising clinical psychologist, writes, 'One issue that is sometimes brought up is the fear that a gay parent may molest their child. This fear is largely due, I believe, to the stereotypes and misinformation that surround homosexuality. In order to shed some light on this topic, I sent a questionnaire to clinical psychologists and child psychiatrists in Orange County, California, asking about their experience with sexual molestation. In this questionnaire, I specifically asked for the sexual orientation of the parent in each case. In over 300 years of accumulated practice, there was not one incident reported of molestation by a lesbian mother or gay father. Every instance of molestation was committed by a heterosexual parent. Respondents included psychologists at the State Hospital who screened specifically for molestation.'

George Weinberg, on a related theme, and speaking with the experience of years of therapeutic practice, identifies another major concern : 'the possibility that children of gay people will grow up to be gay. The scientific studies that have been done on children of gay parents have indicated that this is *not* so. Most homosexuals have had parents who are exclusively heterosexual. As this fact suggests, homosexual men and women do not learn their sexual orientation by imitating their parents. The process by which sexual desires are learned and become distinct is far more complicated than mere imitation.'

Richard Green, Professor in the departments of Psychiatry and Behavioural Science and Psychology at the State University of New York, reinforces this point : 'The lesbian parents I have interviewed have all shown considerable concern and commitment to the well-being of their children. The children have all been psychologically and psychiatrically well-adjusted. The children's sexual identity has followed the majority style, that is the younger children's sex-typed behaviours have been typical for their sex and age, and the older children's sexual behaviours have been heterosexual.' Further, in his 1978 paper, 'Sexual Identity of 37 Children Raised by Homosexual or Transsexual Parents', Dr Green reaches the following interesting conclusion : 'One explanation may be that children do not live in a universe composed entirely of their home environment. . . . We do not know how much parental style contributes to a child's style of psychosexual development, but clearly it is not the only contributing factor.' The influence of the home may not be as all-pervasive as traditional social scientists have led us to believe.

Medical and psychological research, to date, has not yielded any data which might suggest that lesbians ought not to be mothers. The religions, the other body which directs our social thinking, have remained more or less silent on the subject of lesbian mothers. But there are signs that the acceptance of homosexuality, as such, is nearly accomplished. The Catholic Church, for so long a conservative mentor of public morality, has been under pressure to reconsider its teaching. The British Catholic

Social Welfare Commission, for example has made the following
points:

(a) It is untrue to say that every homosexual is attracted to
    children and adolescents and wishes to have physical con-
tact with them. There are, of course, heterosexuals with the
same inclinations. In fact, it would seem that proportionately
to their numbers in the population, the heterosexuals are more
prone to child molestation than homosexuals.

(b) It is inaccurate to claim that all male homosexuals are
    easily identifiable as effeminate or all female homosexuals
as masculine.

(c) It is misleading to say that homosexuals automatically
    recognise each other and form quasi secret societies.

(d) It is untrue that homosexual persons are automatically
    unstable or promiscuous. They are, in fact, quite capable
of forming good relationships which are lasting.

(e) It is a generalisation to claim that homosexual people
    simply require will-power to correct their condition. There
is no easy method of transition from the state of homosexuality to that of heterosexuality; as yet no consistent and
reliable method of transference is known. The invert homosexual must not therefore be too readily blamed if he or she
is hesitant about any attempt to adjust.

(f) Homosexuality is often thought to be anti-family – a threat
    to the institution of the family itself. Some organisations
do, in fact threaten family life in the form in which we understand it today, but other homosexual organisations expressly
aim to promote traditional, accepted standards. There is a
danger of our identifying all homosexuals with radical and
progressive pressure groups.

(g) It is incorrect to claim that homosexuals have a high in-
    cidence of mental disorder. This is simply not borne out
by research.

(h) It is inaccurate to assert that homosexual persons are
    limited to certain social classes or professions. The evidence
of the Wolfenden Report . . . suggests otherwise.

The Commission goes on to say that 'Marriage has not proved

to be a successful answer for most homosexuals. Marriage in these circumstances can be unfair to the partner and even extend the distress of the homosexual to the whole family. It may be marriage for the wrong reasons and, in any case, marriage must not be thought of as the only gateway to God and the only way to fulfilment. . . . The Church has a serious responsibility to work towards the elimination of any injustices perpetrated on homosexuals by society. As a group that has suffered more than its share of oppression and contempt, the homosexual community has particular claim upon the concern of the Church. Homo-sexuals have a right to enlightened and effective pastoral care with pastoral ministers who are properly trained to meet their pastoral needs.'

The first step in our re-education, then, is to understand that homosexual people are not significantly different from heter-osexual people, either in their sexual physiology or in their moral attitudes. The second step is to realize that the human reproduc-tive functions are as available to homosexual people as they are to heterosexuals and that lesbian mothers in particular are endowed with the same maternal skills, or inadequacies, as non-lesbian mothers.

The chief purpose of this book, however, is not to plead for tolerance and charity to be shown towards an afflicted minority group. There are no reasons to suggest that lesbians, because of their lesbianism, are afflicted, and there are equally no reasons why they should be thought of as inadequate enough to need charity. Lesbian mothers with their lovers and children do, indeed, form an invisible outsider group – one which can and does provide a critique of the majority practice. Nearly all our children, at the present time, are still reared within the structure of the traditional nuclear family of husband, wife and children, a structure which has been institutionalized and endorsed by the legislators of our society. By looking at the alternative models provided by lesbians, it is easier to see some of the inadequacies and aberrations typical of the nuclear family. As the Danish writer Suzanne Brøgger, puts it : '. . . still most people stick with the marriage stoically FOR THE SAKE OF THE CHILDREN. But the pathetic fact is that nuclear families in general are unfit to care for children. According to several studies made by the National

Institute of Mental Health in the United States, most married couples should not have children. Divorces occur most frequently where there are children. Childless marriages are the happiest, and every additional child represents an added danger to marital well being. This does not mean that ALL parents are unhappily married. Some of them ARE happy and ought to have children, but these comprised only about 13 to 17 per cent of the couples in the sample.'

The concept of the lesbian family does not mean the rejection of men as individual human beings; if it did, it would not, of course, embody an alternative at all. The children of lesbian mothers are evidence enough that lesbians can, and do, engage with men in a variety of different ways. There is no necessary rejection of individual men; there is, however, a positive rejection of the system of patriarchy. Each person introduced in this book has given her or his feelings and ideas from the point of view of psychological subjectivity – indeed, many of the people, when asked, denied that their life-style had any social or political meaning. They preferred, as would most people, to view their private lives as a matter of personal choice and experience. Nevertheless, taken together and projected to include all those who have not appeared in these pages, the experiences of these people highlight anti-patriarchal themes common to them all. Whether or not the individual women liked individual men, they prized their independence from men : they prized their financial independence, the priority of their claims over their children, their freedom to function in society without the status, or handicap, of 'married women' and their ability to form fulfilling sexual relationships beyond the patronage, domination, or protection, of men.

Lesbian families, by their very existence, demonstrate a rejection of what feminists call rape – that is, they reject any intercourse, social or sexual, which is forced on a woman by a man against her will. When this kind of domination occurs simply because one individual is a man and the other a woman, it is deplored theoretically by all humanitarians, but lesbian families go further by deploring it in practice. The rejection of patriarchal behaviour is the rejection of any perceptions, opinions, actions, customs or rituals which are generated from the premise of male authority. Lesbian families do, in the words of the

Catholic Commission, 'threaten family life in the form in which we understand it today', but the threat is positive, since it implies not the total dismissal of the male but his removal from the position of 'head of the household' to a position of de-institutionalized co-operation – to a position, that is, worked out privately in each relationship according to the terms of human friendship. Masters and Johnson say quite explicitly in *Homosexuality in Perspective* that the present state of our knowledge about human sexuality must bring the greatest degree of pressure to bear on the heterosexual male: 'Of equal importance to the foreseeable increased acceptance of homosexuality is the fact that the potential of woman's physiologic sexual capacity will have to be acknowledged, accepted, and adjusted to by both men and women in our culture. From a speculative point of view, this leaves the heterosexual male in the pressured circumstances of having to undergo a major cultural alteration from a psychosexual point of view. Whether he adjusts well or cannot withstand the ego shock of role alteration will be a fascinating scene to observe. . . . The male in our culture has the most to gain both physiologically and psychosexually as a full sexual partner. He no longer has a future as the "sex expert". . . . It is primarily the male population, in its refusal to assume a sexual partnership role and to acknowledge woman's inherently high level of sexual capacity, that will provide significant social argument for lesbian commitment.'

The persistence of patriarchy is fundamentally provided for by the marriage certificate. Years ago, Germaine Greer wrote, 'If women are to effect a significant amelioration of their condition it seems obvious that they must refuse to marry . . . if independence is a necessary concomitant of freedom, women must not marry.' To those who are still listening, we wish to repeat and endorse her point. Lesbians have never married – indeed, have never been allowed to marry – each other. That does not mean they have not formed life-long unions; many of them have. Nor does it mean they have all been childless; many of them have not been. A legal marriage must be contracted between people of opposite sexes – but why? There is only one clear and convincing reason, and that is the preservation of the patriarchal order – the social assurance of a wife's fidelity, a father's paternity, a child's legitimacy – and not for the sole reason of procreation.

One radical change in the law would strike at the heart of patriarchy : the abolition of the marriage certificate as a legal document. This would not mean that people would not continue to marry; those who sought the blessing of a religious or social institution on their union would still be free to seek and obtain it – but the State would have no part in what should be essentially a private contract. The State would regard each person as a separate social identity, which is, after all, a fundamental principle of democracy.

Legal marriage is already under severe strain. In February 1980, for example, Dr Mia Kelmer Pringle, a prominent British advocate for the nuclear family, called publicly for a reform of the marriage laws – from the opposing standpoint, but in response to the same evidence. She asked for two different types of marriage to be introduced : a 'short-term' form, which could be easily dissolved, and a 'long-term' form, entailing a commitment for a minimum period of fifteen to twenty years. The 'long-term' form would be used by people who had children together and would be more or less impossible to dissolve.

We suggest that there has already been more than enough social experience of trying to force people who become incompatible to stay together 'for the sake of the children'. It is naïve and even careless to suggest that a frustrated and unmotivated couple can provide an adequate environment for the healthy socializing of future citizens. We commend admissions that the present state of the marriage laws is anachronistic and unhelpful, but we urge people to consider that the way forward is not to reform the terms of the marriage certificate, but to abolish it. Lesbians are evidence that people can live together and bring up children without recourse to the marriage certificate. If they can do it, why shouldn't others?

Some may say that this would remove 'freedom of choice'. Others may be outraged that a minority, especially lesbians, should seek to 'impose its will on the majority'. Both responses would be banalities; citizens of democracies long ago accepted the principle of curtailing their individual liberties for the good of the whole community. Earners accept, if grudgingly, that they may not spend every penny they earn as they individually wish, since they allow the State to remove a portion of it as income tax, and have no control over how that money is spent. It is assumed to be spent for the good of the community as a whole. Similarly, in matters of public morality, citizens defer their individual ethics to the legislature; in Britain, for example, the majority of the people still favour capital punishment, but Parliament, rightly, refuses to defer to that wish, using its constituted authority to 'impose' the view that capital punishment cannot be justified. In this way, it is hoped, citizens gradually become re-educated. A government may even declare war, condemning many citizens to certain death, without consulting the wishes of individuals. In matters of domestic living and the upbringing of children, therefore, the State would certainly be entitled to introduce legislation that would help people to adapt better to late-twentieth-century conditions.

Our kinship bonds have been forced apart by industrialization and urbanization. So be it. Our new family groups will not be based on blood, which is, after all, an extremely primitive reason for bonding, but on co-operation and friendship. 'As long as friendship lasts' pledges the quality of the relationship, whereas 'Till death do us part' poses a possibility of living death. A family ought to be thought of, in our own time, as any committed group, whatever their number, age or sex, who share responsibilities. The abolition of the marriage certificate would reduce the importance of the blood bond, eliminate patriarchal privileges in the domestic arena, eliminate the machinery of divorce and child custody as venues for revenge, bitterness and hurt, and, most important of all, give to every citizen the right to be a full, independent member of society.

Lesbian sexuality, as shown by the existence of lesbian families, can provide the basis for a modern life-style. The economic independence of each individual is the primary pre-requisite. Jane, for example, who did not leave Edwin in order to float off into the sunset of 'wedded' bliss with her lesbian lover, had this to say : 'I'm enjoying conducting my own affairs in the way I want them, in the time I want. I enjoy being without hassle, depression and aggro. I enjoy dealing with my own financial matters and spending my money on myself. I don't wish to provide any more. I've done quite enough.'

Her lover, Miriam, added, 'I know Jane resented bitterly the provision of things on her part.' Jane continued, 'I assumed that when we joined forces to each other, that the provisions would have been more equal. I became resentful at being the provider.' We asked why she was so angry about dependence. 'Because it's weak,' she replied. 'I don't like inadequacy. I think once women discover that they can be financially self-supporting, they will automatically become emotionally self-supportive, and not need anybody. I would hazard a guess that I am the sort of person that other people don't like, rather than not liking myself. I should, as a woman, be rather nice, because women are expected to be rather nice. I'm not nice. I'm aggressive. I don't mind being aggressive. I don't mind shouting when there's an injustice. If this gets me disliked – unfortunate, tough. I don't like standard, feminine women who indulge in gossip, intrigue and back-chat.' Did she then, we asked, regard aggression and shouting as masculine characteristics? 'No,' she said. 'I regard them as positive feminine characteristics, which are relatively rare, quite new to the scene and are to do with political feminism.'

In the new order, we hope, relationships will follow the route Jane has pursued. People will come together in freedom and friendship, not because of their financial or emotional needs. For the first time, most women and men will choose their sexual partners on the basis of personal attributes. Inevitably, more women will choose female partners, since homosexuality will be understood to be just as natural as heterosexuality. If lesbian sexuality is threatening now, it can only be for two reasons: either because it shows the possibility of women's sexual independence from men, or because it shows the possibility of women actually liking sex for its own sake and not for the sake of reproduction. Similarly, if lesbian emotionality, which Dr Charlotte Wolff argues to be a deeper reason for bonding between women than sexuality, is felt to be threatening, it can only be because human ties which withstand social ostracism and fear show clearly the power of individuals to resist pressures to conform and obey. When a society perceives a threat to its established norms, it reacts by bringing all possible pressure to bear upon the individuals who do not conform. The reason for a society imposing political norms are obvious enough; less obvious for many people are the reasons why patriarchal society wants to impose sexual norms which can be monitored by the institution of marriage. After all, governments will not fall if one woman goes to bed with her female friend, or even if most women do. No, governments may not fall, but *the family* might. If lesbians are encouraged to form viable domestic units, the nuclear family, taking note of the lesbian alternative, could disappear.

The brave new world we recommend, then, will be one in which relations between the sexes will be based on friendship, co-operation and equality. It will be characterized by the following social aims :

1. All children will be *wanted* children. They will be wanted by at least one adult, of either sex, who will be willing to commit himself or herself to responsible parenting. But the child will also be wanted by the State, because a healthy society will realize that its investment in the future is directly related to its investment in its children. The State – that is, all the citizens – will provide for the economic well-being of all children. This principle is already at work for all non-patriarchally brought-up children : all children who are not paid for by a man are at present paid for by the State, if the single mother claims that right.

2. All variations of family living will be accommodated : one parent of either sex with children; two parents of either sex with children; groups of parents of either sex with children. None of these groupings ought to be institutionalized by law. No one will marry.

3. There will be no such thing as legitimate or illegitimate children. All children will have the same rights under the law.

4. Women will be economically independent from men. Women who choose, therefore, to live with men, will do so freely, not from necessity for security or status. Lesbian unions already demonstrate this practical possibility.

5. Job-sharing, flexi-hours, the sharing of space and facilities, and the sharing of parental responsibilities within larger groups, will enable women to identify themselves as active members of the wider community, without being forced, as they are at present, to choose between motherhood and outside activity – between housework and community work.

6. The separation of sexuality from child-bearing will mean

that sexual relationships will be based on love, care, friendship and other adult capacities, whereas the desire to have a child will come from a person's willingness and desire to mother.

7. The idea of the family will be radically re-thought and re-defined in a more logical way, so that the blood bonds and sexual relationships – the present characteristics of the family – will give way to other characteristics which are primarily social, for example, the shared, voluntary commitment to a dwelling and a life-style. A group of people who *choose* each other, that is, will constitute a family. Each household will be deemed a family.

8. Each individual will earn primarily for his or her own needs. Men will not earn more because they have to 'support a family'. Inequalities in earnings will be compensated for by the State by widening the working of the existing Family Income Supplement and by separate tax assessment. Each individual's partnership with the State will not be muddied by the dependence of some women on some men.

9. Men will be encouraged to mother, equally as are women. If they bring up children, they, too, will be financed by the State to do so.

Some people may recoil with fear at this prospect; others will protest that vast numbers of people are happy with things as they are, so why should they change? We want to say two things about these responses. First, we are not raising the spectre of the totalitarian State. The opposite will be the case. The State will *remove* itself and its legal machinery from the bedroom, where it surely has no place. People's personal relationships will return to being personal and their rights to independence will be protected. Secondly, there is, of course, nothing wrong with being happy, but the personal happiness of some, even of most, ought not to be the guiding vision of a healthy society which is concerned to *improve* itself. It is an old authoritarian argument to say that the peasants were happy with their lot; that slaves were happy with their lot; that workers were happy with their lot; that women were happy with their lot. Yes, many were – they didn't know any better. But gradually, peasants began to want land; slaves began to want freedom; workers began to want power; women began to want the vote and independence. When they wanted these things, they were ridiculed, punished and suppressed until the tide of circumstances carried their claims into the consciousness of the wider community. We are born into change and we adapt, either willingly or resistingly. But in the end, we adapt. Our survival depends on our adaptability. The vote, contraception, education and longevity have changed the circumstances in which Western women live, and with those changed circumstances has come, and will come, a changed consciousness. The death of the old, patriarchal family does not mean the death of our society, of our values, of our aims or of our capacities. It only means the death of the patriarchal family. That ought not to fill us with panic and dread. Love does not die – it finds fresh means of expression.

Instead of spending millions on trying to find out what has gone wrong with the nuclear family, and how to rehabilitate it, we ought to spend those millions on finding out what domestic conditions will suit the people of the future better, and how to achieve them. There ought to be nothing really terrifying about people of the same sex sleeping together, about artificial insemination, about economic independence or about households based on friendship.

To see more clearly what sort of muddle we are in at present, we can look again at the family headed by Jane and Edwin, this time from the outside. Jane carries the labels 'wife', 'mother' and 'lesbian lover'. Edwin carries the labels 'husband', 'father' and 'heterosexual'. Miriam is labelled 'lesbian lover'. Sue's labels are 'daughter' and 'lesbian lover'; Miles' are 'son' and 'heterosexual lover'; and Rae's label is 'daughter'. If Jane's lover, Miriam, is included in the family group, ought not the lovers of Sue and Miles be included as well? Or does family mean all the people who live together under one roof? If it does, then Miriam, Jane's lover, is part of her family, but Edwin, who now lives in a different house, is not. Does family mean people who have a sexual relationship together, excluding incest? If it does, then Edwin and Jane, who used to have a sexual relationship but do so no longer, used to be a family, and Jane and Miriam, who have a sexual relationship, are a family, but Edwin and Miriam, who, in spite of their friendship, never had a sexual relationship together, have no familial relationship. Further, Miles and his lover, who live under Edwin's roof, would represent another family which would exclude Rae, who has no sexual relationship with either of them. Or would this be called a 'sub-family', or something similar? Equally, Sue and her lover have a sexual relationship together but live under a separate roof. Is their familial status the same, or not the same, as Miles'?

At present, some characterizing marks of a family are biological, for example the blood bond, whereas others are social, for example the legality conferred by the marriage certificate. (Husband and wife, of course, are supposed *not* to be related by blood.) It is assumed that heterosexual intercourse which has a warm emotional context is a good basis for entry into the marriage contract. It is still thought rather nasty to marry for money or property, but that is a middle-class prejudice, since the upper classes have done so for centuries and have taken it for granted that sexual passion has its rightful place *outside* marriage. Once the marriage contract and the heterosexual intercourse are established (and, since the advent of widespread contraceptive use, it is no longer important which comes first), the next step is assumed to be the desire for children. Is a married pair without children a family? At present, it seems so. An unmarried mother with her children is also a family. It is not at all clear, to the average person, whether the biological aspect of sex, or its social aspect, is the more important factor in the definition of a family. It is quite clear, on the other hand, that the reproduction of children is thought of as primarily a biological act and one which always implies the existence of a family. In all possible situations – one-parent mother families; one-parent father families; unmarried mothers with children; unmarried fathers with custody of children; two unmarried biological parents with children; or two married biological parents with children – all of these groupings are called families. Similarly, when the biological bond is legally supplanted by the act of adoption, in any of these groupings, the groups are thought of equally as families. The ownership of children is, at present, the primary characteristic of a family, and whether the ownership is natural (biological) or artificial (legally endorsed) makes no difference to the familial status of the individuals concerned. Since the presence of children is sufficient, at present, to define a family, it would seem superfluous to add the sexual practices of the adults concerned.

Some people might prefer to pretend that lesbian mothers do not exist. They are an added and unnecessary complication. But they do exist, and whether they have reproduced 'naturally' (by heterosexual intercourse) or 'artificially' (by insemination), their children are legitimate or illegitimate depending on their marital status in relation to a man who may or may not be the father of their children. Like all women, only they know how their children were conceived. Some women, and many lesbian mothers are among them, will do almost anything to get a baby. For non-lesbian women, this drive has always been admired as the maternal instinct. When lesbian women exhibit it, by contrast, many people judge it to be a selfish and neurotic drive. This illogical division of the one drive into two separate ones is really a division between the drive for heterosexual intercourse and homosexual intercourse, which ought to be irrelevant. The drive is actually the same – the drive to bear a child. The idea of 'mother', like the idea of sex, has both a biological and a social meaning. The biological meaning must be retained by the female sex, but it seems clear that in cases like the marriage between Edwin and Jane, it is perfectly proper to extend the social meaning of motherhood to the male sex. It is self-evident that children need mothering and there seems no reason why men like Edwin, who wish to express their creativity in this way, should not be encouraged to do so. In the future, hopefully, there will be many more men like Edwin. And many more women like Jane.

Lesbians and non-lesbians now have a choice – not only whether or not to bear children, but in what manner; whether to share the rights and responsibilities with a male partner, with the risk of a broken relationship and a legal battle for custody, or whether to use AID and have the right to independence and guardianship. As this trend carries into the future, court battles in which the participants revile each other's competence in the battle for the ownership of children may come to seem as incredible and abhorrent as the old slave markets. The irony of the legal decisions being made in our own time is highlighted by the following letter from Beryl, whose custody case, fought through the 'seventies, was notorious in the United Kingdom : 'Did you know I have the boys now, and even had my eldest son "Bar-Mitzva'd" at the local synagogue? All that legal wrangle – and after it had all died down, the boys' father remarried and his wife didn't want the kids. Men are so irresponsible! . . . I think the boys are happy to be back and have settled in very well. Actually, I don't see them much except when they troop in with their chums, or to sleep and eat. I gather this is normal! So, what a year. . . .'

Lesbian mothers are ordinary mothers, but they are also extraordinary women, able to resist conformity and to live with change. Might it not be that they, together with their children, lovers and friends, can point the way to a more generous future, in which individual human people, of all ages and of each sex, may live together in all manner of different ways? It should already be possible for all of us, next time any of us sees a mother pushing a pram down the street, not to assume that the woman is a married, non-lesbian mother or that the baby is the offspring of her husband. The woman might be a lesbian madonna with her child.

Bibliography

Abbot, S. and Love, B., *Sappho Was a Right-On Woman: A Liberated View of Lesbianism*, Stein & Day, New York, 1972.

Action for Lesbian Parents, 'The Guide to Gay Custody', London, 1977.

Artificial Insemination: an alternative conception, 1979 Lesbian Health Information Project, c/o San Francisco Women's Centre, 3543 18th Street, San Francisco, California 94110.

Ashdowne-Sharpe, Patricia, *The Single Woman's Guide to Pregnancy and Parenthood*, Penguin, Harmondsworth, 1975.

Blizzard, Joseph, *Blizzard and the Holy Ghost, Artificial Insemination: A Personal Account*, Peter Owen, London, 1977.

Brøgger, Suzanne, *Deliver Us From Love*, translated from the Danish by Thomas Teal, Quartet Books, London, 1977.

Bromwich, P., Kilpatrick, M., and Newton, J. R., 'Artificial Insemination with Frozen Stored Donor Semen', *British Journal of Obstetrics and Gynaecology*, New Series, September 1978, pp. 641-4.

Brudenell, Michael; McLaren, Anne; Short, Roger; and Symonds, Malcolm (eds), *Artificial Insemination*, Proceedings of the Fourth Study Group of the Royal College of Obstetricians and Gynaecologists, R.C.O.G., London, 1976.

Carruthers, G. Barry, 'Andrological Aspects of Sexual Medicine : Artificial Insemination by Donor', *British Journal of Sexual Medicine*, February 1977, pp. 11-18.

Catholic Social Welfare Commission, 'An Introduction to the Pastoral Care of Homosexual People', Catholic Information Services, Abbots Langley, Herts, 1979.

Child Poverty Action Group, *National Welfare Benefits Handbook*, ed. Jo Tunnard and Nicholas Warren, 9th ed., November 1979.

Co Evolution Quarterly, Whole Earth Catalogue, No. 21, Spring 1979, PO Box 428, Sausalito, California 94965.

Davenport, Diana, *One-Parent Families: A Practical Guide to Coping*, Pan, London, 1979.

149

Department of Health and Social Security publications :
  'Catalogue of Social Security Leaflets', NI.146/Nov 78;
  'Which Benefit? 60 ways you can get cash help', FB.2/Nov 78;
  'Social Security Benefit Rates from November 1979', NI.196/Nov
    79;
  'National Insurance Maternity Benefits', NI. 17A/Sept 79;
  'Child Benefit – for all your children', CH.1/Aug 76;
  'Child Benefit increase for one-parent families', CH.11/Nov 78;
  'Family Income Supplement', FIS.1/Nov 78;
  'Help with travelling expenses for hospital patients', H.11/Nov
    78;
  'Free milk and vitamins, glasses, dental treatment, prescriptions.
    How to claim these even if you're not on supplementary
    benefit', M.11/Nov 78;
  'Cash help from supplementary benefit : How to claim if you are
    unemployed', SL.8/Nov 78;
  'Cash help from supplementary benefit : How to claim if you
    are a pensioner or if you are not in full-time work', SB.1/Nov
    78.
Equal Opportunities Commission, 'I want a baby . . . but what
  about my job', A study of maternity rights : effects on equal pay
  and equal opportunities, London, n.d.
Ettorre, E. M., *Lesbians, Women and Society*, Routledge & Kegan
  Paul, London, 1980.
Figes, Eva, *Patriarchal Attitudes*, Faber & Faber, London, 1970.
Firestone, Shulamith, *The Dialectic of Sex: The Case for Feminist
  Revolution*, Jonathan Cape, London, 1971.
Glass, Robert H., 'Sex Preselection', *Obstetrics-Gynaecology*, Vol.
  49, No. 1, January 1977.
Green, Richard, 'Sexual Identity of 37 Children Raised by Homo-
  sexual or Transsexual Parents', *American Journal of Psychiatry*,
  Vol. 135, No. 6, June 1978, pp. 692-7.
Greer, Germaine, *The Female Eunuch*, MacGibbon & Kee, Lon-
  don, 1970.
Hite, Shere, *The Hite Report: A Nationwide Study of Female
  Sexuality*, Macmillan Publishing Co Inc., New York, 1976.
Koedt, Anne; Levine, Ellen; Rapone, Anita (eds), *Radical Femin-
  ism*, Quadrangle Books, New York, 1973.
Lesbian Health Matters, The Santa Cruz Women's Health Centre,
  250 Locust Street, Santa Cruz, California 95060.

Martin, D. and Lyon, P., *Lesbian/Woman*, Bantam Books, New York, 1972.

Masters, William H. and Johnson, Virginia E., *Homosexuality in Perspective*, Little, Brown & Co., Boston, 1979. (A comprehensive bibliography of all the scientific papers of Masters and Johnson can be found, together with a plain-language account of their research, in Ruth and Edward Brecher (eds), *An Analysis of Human Sexual Response*, Panther, London, 1968.)

Millett, Kate, *Sexual Politics*, Rupert Hart-Davis, London, 1971.

Morgan, Robin (ed.), *Sisterhood is Powerful: An Anthology of Writings from the Women's Liberation Movement*, Vintage Books, New York, 1970.

National Council For One-Parent Families, 'One-Parent Families: What it is and what it does', London, n.d.

——, 'Single and Pregnant: A guide to benefits', London, April 1979.

National Gay Task Force, 'Gay Parent Support Packet', n.d., available from NGTF, Room 506, 80 Fifth Avenue, New York, NY 10011.

Pennington, G. W. and Naik, Sandra, 'Donor Insemination: Report of a Two-Year Study', *British Medical Journal*, 21 May, 1977, pp. 1327-30.

Plummer, Kenneth, *Sexual Stigma: An Interactionist Account*, Routledge & Kegan Paul, London, 1975.

Richardson, Diane, 'Do Lesbians make good parents?' *Community Care*, 2 August, 1978, pp. 16-17.

Royal College of Obstetricians and Gynaecologists, 'Recommendations for centres planning to set up an A.I.D. service', London, 1979.

Sherfey, Mary Jane, *The Nature and Evolution of Female Sexuality*, Random House, New York, 1966.

Stewart-Park, A and Cassidy, J., *'We're Here': Conversations with Lesbian Women*, Quartet Books, London, 1977.

Wolff, Charlotte, *Love Between Women*, Duckworth, London, 1972.

Wyland, Francie, *Motherhood, Lesbianism and Child Custody*, Wages Due Lesbians, Toronto, and Falling Wall Press, Bristol, 1977.

Index

Other books that will interest you from
ALYSON PUBLICATIONS

Don't miss our FREE BOOK offer at the end of this section!

Beyond the Fragments: **$6.95**
Feminism and the making of socialism
by Sheila Rowbotham, Lynne Segal and Hilary Wainwright

The last decade has seen the women's movement gain strength dramatically among all classes of society. At the same time, the left has too often floundered, as fragmented groups of party liberals and leftists struggle helplessly against a growing right-wing trend.

There's an important reason for all of this, say the authors of *Beyond the Fragments*. It lies in the very different structure of the women's movement as compared to that of most socialist organizations. This new book shows that the left must learn from feminism if it is to become an effective force for grassroots change.

The Men With the Pink Triangle   **$4.95**
by Heinz Heger

For decades, historians have ignored the persecution of homosexuals by the Nazi regime. Now a man who survived six years in the Nazi concentration camps has finally told about that terrible era. *The Men With the Pink Triangle* is the intensely personal story of a Austrian student who was abruptly arrested by the Gestapo in 1939 for being homosexual. He spent the next six years in German concentration camps; like other homosexual prisoners, he was forced to wear a pink triangle on his shirt so he could be readily identified for special mistreatment. His story is one you will never forget. 'One of the Ten Best Books of the Year' (Richard Hall, *The Advocate*).

The Incredible Shrinking American Dream   **$6.95**
by Estelle Carol, Rhoda Grossman and Bob Simpson

History should have been this much fun in high school! The authors have written a comic-book history of the US that will entertain you while it brings to light the often-forgotten history of working people, women and minorities. 'Terrific! A solid class analysis of the American past, in words and pictures that are a delight to the eye and to the funny bone' (Bertell Ollman, creator of the *Class Struggle* game).

Reflections of a Rock Lobster: $4.95
A story about growing up gay
by Aaron Fricke

Aaron Fricke made nationwide news when he took a gay date to his high school prom in Cumberland, Rhode Island. Now he's written the best book ever about growing up gay — about coming to terms with being different, and a lesson in what gay pride can really mean in a small New England town.

Young, Gay and Proud $2.95

One high school student in ten is gay. Here is the first book ever to address the problems and needs of that often-invisible minority, helping young people deal with questions like: Am I really gay? What would my friends think if I told them? Should I tell my parents? Does anybody else feel the way I do?

Fighting Sexual Harassment: An advocacy handbook $3.95
by the Alliance Against Sexual Coercion

This advocacy handbook is for women who have faced sexual harassment at work, and for social service workers whose clients may face such harassment. It includes:
• Myths and facts about sexual harassment;
• How to recognize whether your clients are being harassed;
• Legal options for women who face harassment;
• Other tactics for stopping harassment.

Between Friends $5.95
by Gillian E. Hanscombe

Frances and Meg were friends in school, years ago; now Frances is a married housewife while Meg is involved in lesbian politics. *Between Friends* begins with correspondence between these two women, exploring their feelings about each other, their sexuality and their politics. Soon two other women join the letter-writing: Amy, a feminist who's trying to develop a non-traditional relationship with a man; and Jane, a lesbian separatist. Through their experiences, we see how political beliefs shape our everyday lives. (By the co-author of *Rocking the Cradle*; available August 1982)

BONUS: When you order any three books listed here at the regular price, you may request a *free* copy of any book priced at $4.95 or less.

To order more books:

For more copies of this book, or other books described on the preceding pages, please ask at the bookstore where you bought this copy. We especially encourage you to shop at small, independent bookstores; it is their willingness to carry good but little-known books that makes it possible to publish books such as this one.

If you can't find these books locally, you may order directly from us by mail. Please enclose full payment, and add $.75 postage when ordering just one book. When you order two or more books, we'll pay postage. Add $1.00 for rush or overseas orders.

Bookstores: Standard trade terms apply. Details on request.

Send orders to: **Alyson Publications, Inc.**
PO Box 2783, Dept. B-17
Boston, MA 02208

— — — — — — — — — — — — — — — — — —

Please send me the following books in the quantities indicated:

____Rocking the Cradle ($5.95)

____Beyond the Fragments ($6.95)

____The Men With the Pink Triangle ($4.95)

____The Incredible Shrinking American Dream ($6.95)

____Reflections of a Rock Lobster ($4.95)

____Young, Gay and Proud! ($2.95)

____Fighting Sexual Harassment ($3.95)

____Between Friends ($5.95)

____*Send a free copy of* _____
as offered on the preceding page. I have ordered at least three other books.

Enclosed is my check or money order for $_____.

name: _____

address: _____

city:_____state:_____zip:_____

(Order on your own stationery if you prefer not to cut up this book.)